Strengthening Early Childhood Education and Care in Luxembourg

A FOCUS ON NON-FORMAL EDUCATION

OECD

BETTER POLICIES FOR BETTER LIVES

This work is published under the responsibility of the Secretary-General of the OECD. The opinions expressed and arguments employed herein do not necessarily reflect the official views of the Member countries of the OECD.

This document, as well as any data and map included herein, are without prejudice to the status of or sovereignty over any territory, to the delimitation of international frontiers and boundaries and to the name of any territory, city or area.

The statistical data for Israel are supplied by and under the responsibility of the relevant Israeli authorities. The use of such data by the OECD is without prejudice to the status of the Golan Heights, East Jerusalem and Israeli settlements in the West Bank under the terms of international law.

Please cite this publication as:
OECD (2022), *Strengthening Early Childhood Education and Care in Luxembourg: A Focus on Non-formal Education*, OECD Publishing, Paris, https://doi.org/10.1787/04780b15-en.

ISBN 978-92-64-48205-0 (print)
ISBN 978-92-64-85950-0 (pdf)

Foreword

Early childhood education and care (ECEC) holds immense potential for guiding children towards a positive and rich lifelong learning and development path. There is a need for affordable access for all to ECEC, coupled with the provision of quality services, to ensure that children are met with the best possible start in life.

Historically, policies on ECEC have focused on setting norms to ensure the safety of young children, such as the formulation of standards on buildings, materials or staff-to-child group ratios. However, it is the quality of a child's experience, known as process quality, which matters most for their development, learning and well-being. Fostering process quality involves designing policies in a way that best facilitates meaningful interactions across all ECEC settings. This was the focus of the *Quality beyond Regulations* policy review, which the OECD developed to help countries and jurisdictions better support the different dimensions of quality in ECEC.

Although policies generally focus on child development that takes place within pre-primary education settings and learning environments, a great deal of valuable learning also takes place either deliberately or informally in other less formal settings. Such is the case with ECEC for children in their first years of life, as well as school-aged children during out-of-school hours. Traditionally out of scope in many countries, there is a growing awareness by governments worldwide that the entirety of the ECEC sector needs stronger public investment, supported by policies that help to enhance process quality.

Luxembourg is one such country that is currently driving an ambitious policy agenda for ECEC with a series of critical reforms coming into place in 2022 to improve access, affordability and quality for the country's youngest children. The government reforms are predominantly focused on strengthening what is called non-formal education, which serves young children before compulsory school age (4 years old) and school-aged children during out-of-school hours, to support decades of public investment in pre-primary schools, part of "formal education".

As part of its participation in this project, the Luxembourg government asked the OECD to conduct an in-depth review of the country's ECEC system and the non-formal sector. Workforce development, and quality assurance and improvement are two powerful policy levers that can help drive improvement in the sector and are the main focus of this review. In addition, the review examines Luxembourg's funding model, governance and organisation within the system, as well as equity, access and diversity. It also discusses, to a lesser extent, ECEC within the formal sector, which begins in Luxembourg with an optional year for children at age 3 before two years of compulsory ECEC from age 4.

The ECEC workforce, which encompasses professionals who interact with children and families in ECEC settings, is at the core of the quality of children's experiences within these settings. Raising the professionalisation of the workforce and retaining high-quality staff is a challenge for many countries including Luxembourg. ECEC staff's initial education, professional development and working conditions all matter for the quality of provision, career development and workforce satisfaction, thus making them priorities for reform in Luxembourg. The country also has a highly multilingual and multicultural society, which is reflected at the core of the ECEC system.

In addition, the government is focusing on strengthening its quality assurance and improvement system for non-formal education. In this context, the quality assurance system (e.g. monitoring and inspection) provides important feedback on strengths and weaknesses in the system to inform further actions for improvement. It provides valuable information for ECEC staff and parents to help them evaluate the quality of services when making decisions about their children's early education and care.

The overarching objective of this review is to provide policy recommendations to strengthen the performance of the ECEC system in Luxembourg, in line with national policy goals. The realisation of this report was possible due to the strong engagement of a large range of stakeholders in Luxembourg, as well as the support of the European Commission. The report discusses potential ways to support the ongoing reform agenda and carefully design policies that can lead to meaningful interactions for all children as part of their ECEC experience.

Acknowledgments

This country review of early childhood education and care in Luxembourg is part of the OECD's *Quality beyond Regulations* project undertaken by the Early Childhood and Schools division within the Directorate for Education and Skills. The review involved two policy missions, partly carried out virtually in light of the Covid-19 pandemic (see Annex A for details). The OECD is grateful to all stakeholders who participated in these missions. The insights and opinions of stakeholders provided the OECD team with important contextual information that contributed to the understanding of Luxembourg's Early Childhood Education and Care (ECEC) sector and helped with the formulation of policy recommendations.

The OECD would like to warmly thank Georges Metz and Christine Konsbruck, both from Luxembourg's National Youth Service (*Service National de la Jeunesse* – SNJ), who acted as national co-ordinators for the project, as well as Claude Sevenig from the Ministry of Education, Children and Youth for initiating and supporting the review. Special thanks are given to Claude Bodeving, Monique Collé, Nicole Faber, Linda Ferreira De Almeida, Pit Lutgen, Simone Mortini and Dora Pereira (*Service National de la Jeunesse*), Christiane Meyer, Fabienne Leukart and Maria Ramirez, Lucie Waltzer (*Direction Générale du Secteur de l'Enfance*), Flore Schank (*Direction Générale de l'Enseignement Fondamental*), Tom Muller (*Service de la Formation Professionnelle*), Luc Weis, Elisa Mazzucato (*Service de Coordination de la Recherche et de l'Innovation pédagogiques et technologiques*), Nicole Hekel and Claudine Kirsch (University of Luxembourg) for their support in guiding the work of the review and contributing to its development. The OECD would also like to thank all those who participated in the interviews and meetings during missions or contributed otherwise to the report including representatives from Agence Dageselteren, ECEC providers, parents, and staff and leaders of ECEC settings.

A key part of the preparation of this country review was the development of a country background report on Luxembourg's ECEC system and policies, following guidelines provided by the OECD, and authored by Christine Konsbruck (SNJ) and Flore Schank (*Direction Générale de l'Enseignement Fondamentale*). The country background report is an important output from the review process in its own right as well as the main starting point and resource for the review. The OECD is grateful to the authors of the report.

This report was prepared by the OECD's ECEC team within the Directorate for Education and Skills. The team included Stéphanie Jamet, Victoria Liberatore and Elizabeth Shuey from the OECD, and Katharina Ereky-Stevens and Kathy Sylva from the University of Oxford. The review was led and co-ordinated by Stéphanie Jamet and Victoria Liberatore. The authors of this report are: Chapter 1, Elizabeth Shuey; Chapter 2, Victoria Liberatore; Chapter 3, Katharina Ereky-Stevens and Kathy Sylva. Caroline Cassidy and Alix Got authored the summary of assessments and recommendations, as well as conducted a general review of the report. Caroline Cassidy likewise authored the Foreword and Executive Summary. Alix Got provided research assistance. Julie Harris was in charge of the editing and Eleonore Morena ensured the layout of the report. Throughout the project, Andrea Konstantinidi provided co-ordination support. Alison Burke and Cassandra Davis provided support for production and communication processes.

The review on Luxembourg benefitted from support from the European Commission (EC). The EC took part in virtual missions and commented on drafts of this report. The OECD would like to thank Livia Ruszthy for the co-ordination of the involvement of the EC, and Géraldine Libreau for her contribution to the project.

Table of contents

FIGURES

TABLES

Abbreviations and acronyms

AIM	Access and Inclusion Model (programme in Ireland)
AREG	Regional officers (*agents regionaux*)
ASFT	ASFT Act (*Loi du 8 septembre 1998 réglant les relations entre l'Etat et les organismes oeuvrant dans les domaines social, familial et thérapeutique*)
C1	Proficient level from the Common European Framework of Reference for Languages Competence
CBR	Country Background Report
COVID-19	Coronavirus disease
CPD	Continuous professional development
CSA	Voucher scheme (*chèques-service accueil*)
EC	European Commission
ECEC	Early Childhood Education and Care
ENA	*École Nationale pour Adultes*
ESCS	PISA index of economic, social and cultural status
EYPP	Early Years Pupil Premium (programme in England)
FEDAS	*Fédération des Acteurs du Secteur Social au Luxembourg*
GDP	Gross Domestic Product
IFEN	National Institute for Continuous Professional Development (*Institut de Formation de l'Éducation Nationale*)
ISCED	International Standard Classification of Education
ITM	*Institut du Travail et des Mines*
LTPES	*Lycée Technique pour Professions Educatives et Sociales*
MENJE	Ministry of Education, Childhood and Youth (*Ministère de l'Éducation nationale, de l'Enfance et de la Jeunesse*)
OECD	Organisation for Economic Co-operation and Development
PISA	OECD Programme for International Student Assessment
PPP	Purchasing Power Parity
SCRIPT	Service for Co-ordination of Research and Innovation in Pedagogy and Technologies (*Service de Co-ordination de la Recherche et de l'Innovation pédagogiques et technologiques*)
SEA	Centre-based settings in the non-formal sector (*service d'éducation et d'accueil*)
SNJ	National Youth Service (*Service National de la Jeunesse*)
SPARK	Singapore Preschool Accreditation Framework
TALIS	OECD Teaching and Learning International Survey
USD	United States Dollar

Executive summary

Luxembourg is driving an ambitious early childhood education and care (ECEC) policy agenda. The government has recently initiated a series of critical reforms to improve access, affordability and quality for the country's youngest children. This follows decades of substantial public investment in the ECEC system – particularly in the schooling system to ensure free access for families.

In recent years, the priority has focussed on non-formal education, which in this context is defined as ECEC that serves young children before compulsory school age (4 years old) and school-aged children during out-of-school hours. Key to the reforms has been boosting public investment, developing multilingual education and improving governance and co-ordination across key institutions that oversee formal and non-formal education. The government continues to make adjustments to the system and wishes to strengthen the professional development of the non-formal sector workforce.

This review sets out the Luxembourg context and ECEC policy reforms, focusing on non-formal education. It outlines areas of focus for Luxembourg policy to drive improvement to and build quality ECEC for all.

Governance, funding and equity

Luxembourg has some of the most affordable ECEC among OECD countries, with both free and subsidised ECEC available to families. Participation in ECEC is also widespread. In 2019, approximately 61% of children under age 3 were enrolled in ECEC in Luxembourg, which is above the OECD average.

Nonetheless, despite overall strong investment in ECEC in Luxembourg, clear divisions in the sector (formal versus non-formal and contracted versus non-contracted) contribute to an array of unevenly resourced services, leading to uneven quality beyond minimum requirements, particularly in non-formal education. The current non-formal sector funding scheme may also undermine equity in the system. Prioritising investments in quality improvement for settings, particularly with children from socially or economically disadvantaged and language minority backgrounds, will be key.

In 2013, the government integrated non-formal and formal education into one ministry – the Ministry of Education, Children and Youth (MENJE). This move signalled a recognition of the non-formal sector as a core component of education rather than simply a work support for parents.

MENJE brings together curriculum frameworks, programmes and systems of accountability, improvement and quality assurance from both sectors. However, it still faces some co-ordination challenges and needs to build better links internally to move toward more unified ECEC. Strengthening communication and collaboration across departments and building mechanisms for learning from mutual experience are essential to efficiently capitalising on Luxembourg's investments in ECEC.

Workforce development

Workforce development can help drive improvement in the quality of ECEC provision. Workforce preparedness, ongoing professional development and working conditions are key to boosting staff practices and improving children's experiences.

Higher qualified and better-prepared staff tend to concentrate in the formal sector, which means there is a pressing need for qualified staff in non-formal education. One way to address this is to develop ECEC-specific qualifications and programmes to better prepare new staff and encourage existing ECEC staff in the non-formal sector to advance towards higher levels of qualification. The curriculum framework for non-formal education is a milestone for the sector, but further efforts are needed to prepare staff to implement it.

Continuous professional development is also particularly important in Luxembourg, where staff in the non-formal sector come from different backgrounds and have diverse qualifications. A new reform makes continuous training, coaching and mentoring free of charge for all settings of the non-formal sector. This may help reduce the disparity between the two sectors and support continuous professional development in non-contracted (delivered by for-profit providers) and small settings.

The 2022 reform also seeks to better tailor training content to staff and leader needs. Care needs to be taken to ensure that mechanisms are in place to assess different needs and strengthen the monitoring of the quality of professional development provision. Training also needs to be available in different languages, formats, and to include mechanisms to raise staff qualifications formally. Improving training in these ways could increase the quality of professional development while providing incentives to staff to gain higher qualifications and wages.

In the non-formal sector, attracting and retaining highly-qualified staff is particularly challenging for non-contracted settings, as they can offer less advantageous working conditions than contracted settings (delivered mainly by municipalities or non-profit organisations). The government will also need to review the funding and monitoring systems to support an alignment of wages with qualifications and roles.

Quality assurance and improvement

A national quality assurance and improvement system for ECEC already exists for all types of ECEC provision in Luxembourg, but recent and ongoing government reforms focus on enhancing it for non-formal education.

Regional officers (e.g. "inspectors" for non-formal education) play a vital role in strengthening knowledge on process quality and steering improvement in this sector. To support their role, the government has just introduced new guidelines for monitoring procedures. Ensuring that regional officers also have access to a diverse range of information sources during visits, e.g. information from discussions with staff members, is important to help strengthen their ability to foster quality improvement. Other options could include introducing systematic observations of staff and children during everyday activities and providing additional training to strengthen regional officers' ECEC-specific knowledge.

A risk-based approach to monitoring visits would ensure that efforts are proportionate and focussed on where they can have the greatest impact. Such an approach could free up regional officers to focus on the follow up of improvement plans with settings and include observations in their visits.

Clarifying the role of the two monitoring agencies for non-formal ECEC will enhance the work of both and could strengthen the mechanisms to support quality improvement. The government has already started this process. Adjustments include improved communications around both agencies' control versus support functions to build a balance between the two and not undermine relationships with ECEC settings.

Reflective practice is one of the cornerstones of Luxembourg's quality assurance system. In particular, self-evaluations are increasingly seen as key to ensuring quality of provision. However, wider staff participation within settings beyond centre leaders could be encouraged to support reflection and seek team improvement.

Analysing data on the non-formal sector will also be critical to assessing whether the Luxembourg ECEC system is accessible to families and of high quality. How this data is combined and shared with stakeholders is also important to help channel resources and monitoring efforts, for example.

Finally, parents and children could become more active stakeholders in the quality improvement process in non-formal ECEC. This includes incorporating their feedback into the system and sharing data with them regularly.

Assessment and recommendations

Governance, funding and equity

Luxembourg's substantial investment in early childhood education and care reflects its long-term commitment to providing access to all children

The Luxembourg government has a long-term commitment to ensuring greater access for all children across society to early childhood education and care (ECEC). This is split between the schooling system or formal sector, and the non-formal sector, which serves young children before compulsory school age (4 years old) and school-aged children during out-of-school hours.

In 2009, the government introduced a subsidy funding scheme (*chèques-service accueil*, CSA) for non-formal education to increase access to high-quality ECEC and to advance goals to improve equity. The scheme grants price reductions to families according to their household incomes and composition. All children aged 0-12 living in Luxembourg and children from cross-border families with one of the parents working in Luxembourg can benefit from the CSA. As a result, the non-formal sector has expanded considerably, with contracted places for children (delivered mainly by municipalities or non-profit organisations) more than doubling between 2009 and 2019. Non-contracted places (delivered by for-profit providers) have also grown more than five times in the same period.

Free access to pre-primary education is also long-standing in Luxembourg. Recently, the government has explored ways to extend this to the non-formal sector. As of 2017, all children from age 1 to 4 benefit from 20 free hours per week (if in ECEC centres), as well as the subsidy funding scheme. In 2022, out-of-school services will also be free to families from 7:00 a.m. to 7:00 p.m. on school days.

In 2019, approximately 61% of children under age 3 were enrolled in non-formal ECEC in Luxembourg, which is above the OECD average of 25% for participation in ISCED 0. Furthermore, 87% of children aged 3-5 were enrolled in the ECEC sector in 2018.

The Ministry of Education, Childhood and Youth could strengthen collaboration and promote best practices across ECEC departments

In 2013, non-formal ECEC was integrated into the Ministry of Education, Children and Youth (MENJE) to bring together all programmes and support a coherent system of accountability and quality improvement. Consequently, the single ministry has aligned and developed complementary curriculum frameworks for both sectors. This includes an ambitious curriculum framework for non-formal ECEC that complements the formal education curriculum. Furthermore, the compulsory framework includes a major focus on multilingualism through an innovative approach, a flagship of Luxembourgish education and culture. A comprehensive quality assurance system was also developed to support the framework.

However, MENJE faces some co-ordination challenges between formal and non-formal education departments, including assigning responsibilities, building workforces and creating approaches to quality monitoring. Strengthening communication across departments and building mechanisms for learning from mutual experience are essential to efficiently capitalising on Luxembourg's investments in ECEC.

Many areas could benefit from greater collaboration, especially in a time of pedagogical innovation and ongoing reforms within the non-formal sector. Sharing feedback on multilingual programmes, parents' participation, in-service training and monitoring would help foster a common culture and vision and contribute to achieving high-quality ECEC. MENJE needs to ensure that all efforts for both sectors are bi-directional, equally valued and mutually recognised and implemented.

> *Recommendations:*
>
> *Strengthen co-ordination across departments within the Ministry of Education, Children and Youth.*
>
> *Develop mechanisms to support stronger communication and alignment across departments with responsibility for the formal and non-formal sectors.*
>
> *Bring together knowledge on ECEC quality across the formal and non-formal sectors to build collaboration and create connections for children and families.*

The current non-formal sector funding scheme creates disparities in quality and may undermine equity

In the non-formal sector, the funding scheme differs depending on whether the status of the provider is "contracted" or "non-contracted" ("*conventionné*" or "*non-conventionné*"). While contracted providers refer to historic providers, non-profit organisations or municipalities, non-contracted status concerns mostly for-profit providers.

Both types of providers are eligible for the subsidy funding scheme, but contracted providers receive additional funding from the government, while non-contracted providers rely more heavily on parental participation.

In 2022, the expansion of continuous professional development funding for ECEC staff in the non-contracted sector is a step towards reducing the gap in funding. However, parental fees remain unregulated in the non-contracted sector, whereas they are capped at the amount of the CSA (EUR 6 per hour) for contracted providers.

The 20 free hours measure has, however, introduced more equity in the system. Nevertheless, parents with low incomes who need more than 20 hours per week or care for children younger than 1 year may still have to pay extra fees in non-contracted settings. In contracted settings, access can be entirely free for children older than 1 year. Price differences may lead families to choose a setting according to their background and could directly impact social mixing.

Significantly lower staff wages in the non-contracted sector are also an issue, leading to difficulties in attracting and retaining qualified staff (especially staff who speak Luxembourgish). High turnover and low-qualified staff directly affect the quality of the provision of the curriculum and multilingual programme. Ensuring that all types of ECEC are of high quality is foundational for building equity.

In-depth analysis needs to be conducted to better understand how the funding scheme plays a role in the disparities in quality and equity beyond the minimum requirements that need to be fulfilled, or if those disparities are inherent to the split between the contracted and non-contracted parts of the sector. This includes collecting and analysing data on the cost of ECEC provision in the non-contracted sector and resources such as parental fees to understand why certain settings offer wages below those of the contracted sector. Depending on the findings, the allocation of public investment between contracted and non-contracted settings might need to be revisited. Additional support for key policy goals, such as the multilingual programme, might need to be more carefully targeted to ECEC settings serving children from socio-economically disadvantaged and language minority backgrounds.

The monitoring system also plays a vital role in ensuring that public funding translates into high quality across the sector and incentivises wage increases in non-contracted settings to foster staff retention and high-quality ECEC.

> ### Recommendations:
>
> *Investigate the costs of providing high-quality ECEC and ensure investments are allocated efficiently across different types of ECEC provision, particularly in the non-formal sector between contracted and non-contracted settings.*
>
> *Prioritise investments in quality improvement for settings serving larger numbers of children from socio-economically disadvantaged and language minority backgrounds.*

Workforce development

The development of ECEC-specific qualifications and programmes would help address the pressing need for qualified staff in the non-formal sector

ECEC professionals are key agents in supporting the quality of the ECEC system and shaping children's learning, development and well-being. By law, Luxembourg requires specific ECEC staff qualifications, but there is significant variation between the formal and non-formal sectors. In non-formal ECEC, only 60% of staff need to hold a minimum ISCED Level 3 qualification in social or educational sciences, which is a relatively low level of qualification. In formal ECEC, teachers are required to have a bachelor's qualification (ISCED Level 6) in educational sciences or an equivalent qualification from abroad.

The ECEC workforce can choose between three Luxembourgish staff training degrees, but none of these has a strong focus on ECEC, and all of them cover all age groups under 12. The two degrees targeting the non-formal sector have a broad focus on social work. Additionally, in pre-training for both the formal and non-formal sectors, teachers and staff are not familiarised with the non-formal sector curriculum framework.

Creating specialised programmes would better prepare new staff to implement the non-formal curriculum framework and could allow existing ECEC staff to advance towards higher levels of qualification. The MENJE is working to implement a new one-year vocational training diploma (ISCED Level 3) starting in September 2022, focusing specifically on ECEC in the non-formal sector. The programme would target students who graduated from secondary school, home-based providers and working adults with no qualifications. The aim is to strengthen their skills and knowledge and thus the quality of their interactions with children, and facilitate their career progression.

Introducing additional specialised programmes at higher education levels (ISCED Levels 4 and 5) would also help to better distinguish between different roles and responsibilities such as leadership functions or cross-functional pedagogical tasks for pedagogical referents of the multilingual programme.

Other potential options include introducing specialisation in ECEC for the upper secondary (ISCED Level 3) qualification programme in the social field or adding years for specialisation that could lead to diplomas at higher levels of education.

To better prepare the workforce, there also needs to be more practical ECEC experience during initial training and familiarisation with the non-formal sector curriculum. All this could also help to ensure a smoother transition for children between non-formal and formal education.

Recommendations:

Strengthen the integration of the national ECEC curriculum frameworks into initial education programmes (ISCED Levels 3 and 6 degrees).

Explore the possibility of developing ECEC-specific initial education programmes that provide qualifications at various levels of education (ISCED Levels 4 and 5).

Consider the possibility of introducing specialisation in ECEC in the upper secondary (ISCED Level 3) qualification programme (Lycée Technique pour Professions Educatives et Sociales).

Continuous professional development for staff and leaders in non-formal education is central to the government's ambitious 2022 reform

Continuous professional development is an important way to help strengthen the competencies and knowledge of the non-formal education staff in Luxembourg. The sector currently faces significant variation in staff qualification levels and types. In 2016 MENJE enforced minimum continuous professional development requirements for ECEC providers to be eligible for the subsidy scheme. As part of the 2022 reforms, the government is now seeking to tackle uneven participation in training and raise the quality of training in the non-formal sector. This includes revisiting the content and format of courses and developing training offers for leaders as well. Training will also be freely accessible to ECEC staff and leaders from both contracted and non-contracted providers.

Each setting will be granted a credit of training hours (equivalent to 24 hours per full-time staff) that may be adapted to the needs of each staff member (including leaders and staff not working directly with children) insofar as legal requirements per staff are respected.

The government's sponsorship of training courses in all types of settings can help to reduce the disparity between the two sectors and support continuous professional development in non-contracted and small settings. Additionally, the inclusion of home-based providers in the plan is an important step in professionalising the non-formal sector and advancing skills.

The remaining barriers for staff to attend training include the need for providers to cover for staff time and difficulties finding replacements for staff in training.

Recommendation:

Ensure that the reimbursement of the cost of continuous professional development for all types of settings and staff helps reduce the gap in staff preparedness between the contracted and non-contracted sectors.

The focus needs to be on professional development quality, format and links with formal qualifications

The 2022 reform also intends to develop a coherent and diverse set of courses and to adjust the content to staff and leader training needs. Information gathered from site visits and confirmed by a survey issued by the National Youth Service (*Service national de la jeunesse*, SNJ) demonstrate the need for more training on curriculum implementation, particularly for the multilingual programme.

A commission chaired by SNJ, the "Further Training Commission", is charged with overseeing reform of the system, co-ordinating the provision of training from agencies, accrediting course content and trainer qualifications, and ensuring that continuous professional development responds to the needs of the sector.

With this new approach, care needs to be taken to ensure that mechanisms are in place to assess staff and leader training needs and that systematic mechanisms are established to monitor the quality of training provision.

Furthermore, as formats such as mentoring, coaching and group training have been shown to lead to more effective interactions with young children and will benefit from public funding through the reform, the focus needs to be on ensuring that these formats are proposed and used by ECEC centres.

Continuous professional development does not currently provide formal certifications enabling staff to obtain higher qualifications. Doing so could enhance career pathways in Luxembourg and raise the formal qualifications of ECEC staff. This would entail strengthening co-operation between professional development and initial training providers and developing systems of micro-credits for participation in modules. Such a system could both increase the quality of professional development while also providing incentives to staff to participate in acquiring higher qualifications and potentially higher wages.

> *Recommendations:*
>
> *In line with the objectives of the reform, ensure that the offer of continuous professional development responds to staff training needs. It needs also to increase the training offer on curriculum framework implementation, inclusion and multilingual education.*
>
> *Ensure that the reform leads to the provision of training in a diversity of languages and through alternative professional development formats, including mentoring, coaching and induction programmes.*
>
> *Ensure that effective mechanisms for monitoring the quality of professional development provision are in place.*
>
> *Design mechanisms to raise staff qualifications through continuous professional development.*

Differences in working conditions and wages create uneven quality among providers of non-formal education

The plurality of ECEC settings and the status of provision has led to heterogeneous working conditions within the non-formal sector, between contracted and non-contracted settings, and between centre-based staff and home-based providers.

In particular, staff working in contracted settings benefit from a collective pay agreement with regular increases. Staff working in non-contracted settings are only protected by the national minimum wage. Wages are also negotiated at a lower level in non-contracted settings.

These disparities translate into differences in staff profiles. Non-contracted settings rely more on a low-qualified and predominantly foreign workforce. This makes it challenging for non-contracted providers to fulfil the requirement to have a fluent speaker of Luxembourgish on staff and support the multilingual focus of the curriculum.

As discussed above, reviewing the funding system and enhancing professional development across the non-formal sector would help to mitigate gaps in wages and qualifications.

Discussions are ongoing to review the status of home-based providers to improve their working conditions and the quality of their services. However, it will be important also to respect the specificity of home-based providers and ensure that the new arrangement provides parents with the flexibility they may seek with home-based provision.

> *Recommendations:*
>
> *Review the funding and monitoring systems to support an alignment of wages with qualifications and roles. Ensure that staff with similar profiles have similar wages in contracted and non-contracted settings within the non-formal sector.*
>
> *To expand the pool of potential candidates for the multilingual pedagogical referents, ensure that staff who need to develop their language skills participate in relevant training.*

Continue discussions in the sector on changing the status of home-based providers to improve their working conditions and the quality of their services.

Quality assurance and improvement

Luxembourg is particularly focused on how to enhance quality assurance and improvement in non-formal education

In Luxembourg, national quality assurance arrangements for ECEC, such as registration, regulation, inspection and quality assurance, exist for all types of ECEC provision, including formal and non-formal education providers, and centre-based as well as home-based provision.

More recently, the country has also made quality assurance in non-formal education central to its ECEC policy. For example, since 2017, the quality assurance system in non-formal education is now linked to the ECEC subsidy scheme. Settings that wish to be recognised by MENJE must meet a number of conditions. These include implementing the national curriculum framework and the multilingual education programme, meeting continuous professional development requirements and accepting regular external evaluations.

The current system also now integrates home-based providers in the quality assurance and improvement for the non-formal sector, where both structural and process aspects of quality are monitored.

Regional officers play a vital role in strengthening knowledge on process quality in non-formal education

ECEC providers of non-formal education are supported by a team of 32 regional officers working under SNJ to focus on process quality and improvement of care. This complements the existing body of MENJE inspectors, who are predominantly focused on structural quality and compliance with regulatory standards.

Regional officers are trained to exchange with settings and explore pedagogical approaches and practices. However, as the curriculum framework for non-formal education is relatively new and regional officers are also new to their jobs, there is still a period of adjustment. Regional officers rely heavily on discussions with the centre leader, analysis of documents prepared in advance of visits and the quality of the physical environment.

New guidelines for monitoring procedures were introduced at the end of 2021, with a stronger focus on pedagogical approaches, setting environment and materials, staff-child interactions, interactions with parents and the quality of management. In addition, indicators have been developed for each area to help regional officers in their evaluations.

There are other ways that the framework could be enhanced to strengthen knowledge on process quality. For example, ensuring that regional officers have a diverse range of information sources during their visits, such as information from discussions with staff members on the challenges they face when implementing the curriculum framework. Other options could include the introduction of systematic observations of staff and children during everyday activities.

Recommendations:

Engage ECEC staff, parents and children in monitoring visits to broaden and deepen knowledge of process quality.

Develop systematic observations of staff interactions with children as well as children's interactions with one another, and introduce observational monitoring tools to assess process quality.

Further training would strengthen regional officers' ability to foster quality improvement

It is important that as the curriculum framework continues to evolve, there is a continuous focus on supporting interactions that foster child well-being and development, such as socio-emotional skills, emotional resilience, use of multiple languages and respect for diversity.

SNJ has paid specific attention to building regional officer team capacity. Each regional officer needs to hold a master's degree in pedagogics or equivalent, receive two months of initial training and be regularly monitored by two co-ordinators.

However, regional officers do not necessarily have specific experience or training in child education or ECEC. As the system is still relatively new, delivering sound advice in terms of pedagogy, meaningful interactions and curriculum implementation can still be a challenge.

Regional officers also need to have a greater knowledge or experience of ECEC through further training and/or work experience. This would help to deepen their understanding of ECEC quality implementation and provide feedback to settings that is linked to their assessment results.

Providing feedback to centre leaders and helping design self-improvement strategies are two other ways to improve the system.

> *Recommendation:*
>
> *Offer further training for regional officers on making recommendations for improvement and supporting providers to draw up their own self-improvement plans.*

Reflective practice is one of the cornerstones of Luxembourg's quality assurance system, but greater staff participation within settings could be encouraged

Self-evaluations are internationally recognised as key to ensuring quality of provision in the ECEC sector. The Luxembourgish assurance quality system for non-formal education includes the documentation of practices by centre staff in a logbook and other self-assessment measures. Nevertheless, centre leaders often carry out self-assessments, thus not reflecting the voice of all staff.

As indicators are being developed to guide ECEC settings, it will be important that new tools for self-reflection are used by a range of ECEC staff with different backgrounds and experiences in self-assessment processes. Centre leaders could also share results of external monitoring more widely with staff and involve them in designing improvement plans.

Documenting children's learning journeys would also offer a valuable opportunity to engage with parents and enhance communication with schools for children enrolled in formal education. For example, monitoring an individual child's multilingual learning experience could be useful and strengthen parent-ECEC provider relationships.

> *Recommendations:*
>
> *Encourage centre leaders to share the results of external monitoring with ECEC staff members and involve staff in designing improvement plans. Strengthen the capacity of the staff to undertake self-evaluation.*
>
> *Introduce recommendations for ECEC staff to document children's engagement in learning experiences to aid identification of children's needs and interests, and communicate this to parents and schools for children enrolled in formal education.*

The effectiveness of the non-formal sector monitoring system could be enhanced with increased co-ordination between agencies and a risk-based approach

Luxembourg is striving for a clearer separation between the monitoring purposes of control versus support in quality improvement by separating inspector responsibilities between the Department for Children and SNJ. However, there are certain overlaps in their roles, causing some tensions, particularly in relation to the role of regional officers.

The government has clarified the responsibilities between the two monitoring bodies for the non-formal sector and released regional officers from some duties to monitor compliance. However, co-operation can be further strengthened, especially in the case of a continued breach of regulations, to ensure that providers address concerns of non-compliance. Furthermore, if the control function of regional officers is further reduced, MENJE will need to further consider the role of its agents (Department for Children) in monitoring compliance with regulations.

Tailoring monitoring efforts to the needs of providers may also enhance the efficiency of processes. A risk-based approach to monitoring visits ensures that efforts are proportionate and focussed on where they can have the greatest impact. Such an approach could free up regional officers to focus on the follow-up of improvement plans with settings and include observations in their visits.

Professional development is one area that could benefit from enhanced monitoring. If results on quality are shared with educational training institutions and external training agencies, in-service and pre-service training can then be adapted accordingly to meet the professional and practical needs of staff.

> *Recommendations:*
>
> *Improve communication of the new responsibilities of the two monitoring bodies in their roles of control versus support to enhance the work of both, and the capacities of regional officers to support quality improvement in the sector.*
>
> *Review the steps available to put in place when a provider consistently falls short of expected levels of quality.*
>
> *Investigate better ways to channel information about gaps in process quality to the training institutions so that monitoring feeds directly into future in-service and pre-service training.*
>
> *Consider using monitoring results to adopt a risk-based, proportionate approach to monitoring visit programming, which will help channel monitoring resources.*

A range of data is being collected but could be shared and combined more effectively to inform and support the quality and equity of the system

Assessing whether the Luxembourg ECEC system is accessible and high-quality requires access to a wide range of data. For non-formal education, efforts are made to link data collected from registration processes, structural quality monitoring and process quality monitoring results. The integration of further quantitative data on enrolment, staffing and users of ECEC should also be considered.

The linking of quantitative data, together with monitoring process outcomes, can provide valuable evidence of the strengths and weaknesses of the ECEC system to help identify gaps that need to be addressed and further guide policy development.

For example, understanding patterns of ECEC participation among families according to their income or language profiles can help focus human and financial resources, particularly to support equity and multilingual ambitions.

When building the platform, attention should be given to how much additional workload is created both internally and for providers. In addition, steps will be needed to ensure data reliability and to assign responsibility within MENJE for carrying out data analysis.

Recommendations:

Prioritise work on the centrally organised, systematic collection of information on the sufficiency of ECEC provision, characteristics of children and families participating in ECEC and the diversity of the workforce, including the language profiles of children, families and staff.

Use data to identify patterns of ECEC participation among diverse families, including use of home-based versus centre-based ECEC, enrolment in contracted versus non-contracted settings, as well as reasons for forgoing participation in the first year of formal education (éducation précoce).

Parents and children could become active stakeholders in the quality improvement process

In Luxembourg, parents are viewed as key partners in ECEC settings, and their involvement in sharing their languages and cultures is a core pillar of the multilingual programme. Therefore, discussing with users and hearing their voices is crucial to building an ECEC system that addresses their needs and expectations and reflects the diversity of families and children in the country.

The 2021 revision of the curriculum framework, as well as the publication of materials targeted to parents, are noteworthy examples of how SNJ is trying to enhance accessibility and understanding of the curriculum framework. SNJ could also more actively engage families in the process of reviewing the curriculum framework and creating resources for families.

Engagement with families, particularly on the educational objectives of the non-formal sector, should also include those with children not currently in the system.

Monitoring can further contribute to quality improvement if monitoring results are shared with parents. At a setting's level, parents can provide valuable feedback on the quality of ECEC provision and their understanding of the curriculum framework. Visits of regional officers could also include discussions with parents and feedback from parental surveys. Luxembourg currently has plans to introduce a mandatory parent council for non-formal education at the national level, which could help build greater parental involvement.

Recommendations:

Continue to inform the public about the educational objectives of the non-formal sector, including through outreach to families who are not engaged with this system.

Increase the possibilities for parental engagement and involvement in non-formal ECEC by creating clear expectations for the sector to prioritise this dimension of quality.

Introduce a requirement to publish (for example, on a parent portal or through formal communication to a structure's "parent committee") condensed information on the monitoring results (e.g. improvement plans and progress towards achieving goals).

1 Context of the review

This chapter examines Luxembourg's early childhood education and care (ECEC) system, its main strengths and challenges and makes recommendations to inform discussions on ongoing and future policy developments. This includes an overview of the system's governance and organisation, with particular attention to the non-formal education sector. Issues of funding, access and equity within Luxembourg's ECEC system and the government's current reform agenda are also explored.

The OECD *Quality beyond Regulations* project

Early childhood education and care (ECEC) holds tremendous potential for children, families and societies when it is of high quality. High-quality ECEC is foundational for children's development, learning and well-being and supports children's outcomes later in life, including school performance, labour market participation and physical and mental health. Moreover, quality ECEC can foster increased intergenerational social mobility, social integration and poverty reduction (OECD, 2018[1]). Children from disadvantaged socio-economic backgrounds, in particular, can benefit from high-quality ECEC.

The OECD's *Quality beyond Regulations* policy review supports countries and jurisdictions to better understand the different dimensions of quality in ECEC and the policies that can enhance process quality in particular. As part of its participation in this project, Luxembourg asked the OECD to conduct an in-depth review of their ECEC system, particularly of the non-formal sector. Non-formal education in Luxembourg encompasses ECEC for young children who are not yet enrolled in the formal education system, as well as education and care for school-age children provided outside of school hours (e.g. before- or after-school care). The review focuses on the quality of ECEC in Luxembourg, particularly on policies that can support process quality, emphasising aspects related to workforce development and quality assurance and improvement.

The overarching objective of the review is to provide policy recommendations to strengthen the performance of the ECEC system in Luxembourg in line with national policy goals. The review analyses the strengths and challenges of existing ECEC policies in Luxembourg from a comparative international perspective and provides recommendations for future policy development.

Specific objectives include:

- informing ongoing and future policy design and implementation through recommendations on policy development and guidance on key considerations in view of the national context
- providing an opportunity for Luxembourg to learn from other OECD countries and international good practices to generate new thinking on ECEC quality development.

This first chapter discusses Luxembourg's main strengths and challenges regarding governance and organisation, funding, access, and equity of ECEC. Further, it makes recommendations to inform discussions on ongoing and future policy developments, summarised in Box 1.1. The review took place when Luxembourg was pursuing several reforms of its non-formal education system, including a reform of continuous professional development, revisions of the monitoring framework and changes to the governance of the system. Recommendations made in this chapter and subsequent chapters build on this policy agenda as communicated at the time of writing while indicating areas for additional changes.

Box 1.1. Policy recommendations

Governance and organisation

- Strengthen co-ordination across departments within the Ministry of Education, Children and Youth. Continue increasing collaboration across departments with different licensing, monitoring and quality improvement roles for the non-formal ECEC sector. In addition, develop mechanisms to support stronger communication and alignment across departments with responsibility for the formal and non-formal sectors.
- Build more links between non-formal and formal education to gradually move towards a more unified ECEC sector. This includes creating opportunities for greater movement of staff between the sectors and career progression across the sectors, co-ordinating aspects of the monitoring

---

systems and increasing alignment of the on-the-ground implementation of the different curriculum frameworks. Ensure that requirements for collaboration between formal and non-formal education are included for and implemented by staff, leaders, teachers and administrators in both sectors.

- Strengthen involvement from a range of stakeholders, including children, in policy development and reform processes.

Funding

- Investigate the costs of providing high-quality ECEC and ensure investments are allocated efficiently across different types of ECEC provision, particularly in the non-formal sector between the contracted and non-contracted settings. Create pathways for staff to achieve more advanced qualifications in the non-formal sector, rebalancing salaries in the sector between the contracted and non-contracted, to recognise and incentivise stronger professional training.

- Make funding mechanisms intended to encourage equitable access to ECEC for children from diverse backgrounds, as well as for those who may need extra supports to address specific needs, more visible to ECEC settings, providers of professional development and regional officers.

Equity and inclusion

- Prioritise investments in quality improvement for settings serving larger numbers of children from socio-economically disadvantaged and language minority backgrounds.

- To ensure that all ECEC centres benefit from pedagogical expertise, encourage the use of pedagogical supports through the reform of the continuous professional development system, particularly for small centres that may have difficulty recruiting and retaining pedagogical referents. Consider options for home-based providers to also work with pedagogical referents. Moving in these directions would ensure that children in all types of non-formal ECEC settings benefit fully from the multilingual programme and the robust curriculum framework.

- To expand the pool of potential candidates for the multilingual pedagogical referents, ensure that staff who need to develop their language skills participate in relevant training.

- Continue to inform the public about the educational objectives of the non-formal sector, including through outreach to families who are not yet engaged with this system or who may not be seeking childcare. Increase the possibilities for parental engagement and involvement in non-formal ECEC by creating clear expectations for the sector to prioritise this dimension of quality.

A review of process quality in early childhood education and care in OECD countries

Awareness of the importance of ECEC has grown among policy makers worldwide. In OECD countries, the expansion of provision of pre-primary education (ISCED 02) and targeted measures for children from disadvantaged backgrounds resulted in an increase in enrolment rates, reaching universal or near-universal participation for children aged 3-5 in several countries. In most OECD countries, participation is universal or near-universal in the year before primary school entry, which constitutes significant progress towards the Sustainable Development Goals education targets. As access to ECEC increases, policy makers are shifting their attention to ensuring the quality of provision for all children. In particular, process quality has been identified as the primary driver for children's development in ECEC (Melhuish et al., 2015[2]). Process quality refers to children's experience of ECEC and includes their interactions with other children, staff, space and materials, their families and the wider community.

Despite the growing recognition of the importance of high-quality ECEC, funding for ECEC has remained lower than for later stages of education. On average in 2019, OECD countries spent 0.87% of gross domestic product (GDP) on ECEC as compared to 1.5% and 1.9% of GDP on primary and secondary education, respectively (OECD, 2021[3]). In about half of OECD countries, expenditure on children aged 3-5 enrolled in ECEC as a percentage of GDP decreased between 2013 and 2017 (OECD, 2020[4]). Furthermore, the proportion of private expenditure is higher in pre-primary education than in primary education. More children are enrolled in private institutions in ECEC than in primary and secondary education, which further highlights differences across stages of education (Figure 1.1).

Figure 1.1. Share of enrolment by type of institution and education level, 2019

Average enrolment of children/students in public and private educational settings across OECD countries

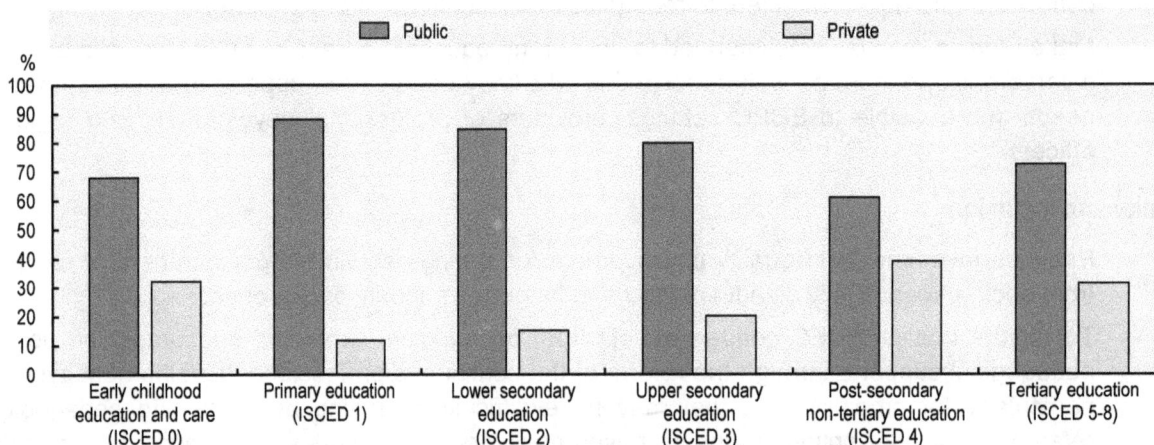

Source: OECD (2021[3]), *Education at a Glance 2021: OECD Indicators*, https://doi.org/10.1787/b35a14e5-en.

In addition, the coronavirus (COVID-19) pandemic has created challenges for the continued operation and funding of ECEC services around the world, which highlighted the importance of ECEC in multiple ways. The need to continue to provide ECEC services to allow parents to go to work became evident, particularly in the case of essential workers. Discussions also centred on the long-term effects for children that the closure of services could imply. Close interactions with educators and peers are essential to provide children with cognitive and emotional support, which can be more challenging to ensure through online platforms than for later stages of education (OECD, 2021[5]). With the COVID-19 pandemic negatively affecting global health, economy and social welfare, government support will be needed to ensure that children have access to quality ECEC despite the challenging context.

The OECD's *Quality beyond Regulations* policy review supports countries and jurisdictions to better understand the different dimensions of quality in ECEC and the policies that can enhance process quality in particular (Box 1.2).

Box 1.2. The *Quality beyond Regulations* project

The *Quality beyond Regulations* policy review was initiated to support countries and jurisdictions to better understand the different dimensions of quality in ECEC, focusing on process quality in particular. The project's first phase culminated in a literature review and meta-analysis of the links between different dimensions of quality and children's learning, development and well-being, published under the title *Engaging Young Children* (OECD, 2018[1]).

The second phase of the project built from this research base to address the overarching question: How can policies enhance process quality and child development, and what are good examples of these policies? To address this question, countries in the OECD's Early Childhood Education and Care Network were invited to share information on relevant policies by completing a questionnaire. Twenty-six countries responded to this invitation, resulting in a rich database of information on ECEC systems around the world and their efforts to promote high-quality ECEC as of the year 2019.

In addition, six countries (Australia, Canada, Ireland, Japan, Luxembourg and Switzerland) participated in the *Quality beyond Regulations* project by completing in-depth country background reports. These reports were undertaken by national governments, as well as provincial governments in Canada. The reports were based on a common framework developed by the OECD to facilitate comparative analysis and maximise the opportunities for countries and jurisdictions to learn from each other. The country background reports were complementary to the information collected in the policy questionnaire. Together, these two sources provided the data for the main analyses of the review.

The project culminated in the publication of the report *Starting Strong VI: Supporting Meaningful Interactions in Early Childhood Education and Care*. In addition, a multidimensional map of policy levers for quality in ECEC was published on an online platform, making available the breadth and depth of policy information that underpins the findings of the Starting Strong VI publication.

Note: The report was published under the below mentioned source. The online platform is found at https://quality-ecec.oecd.org.
Source: (OECD, 2021[6]), *Starting Strong VI: Supporting Meaningful Interactions in Early Childhood Education and Care*, https://doi.org/10.1787/f47a06ae-en.

The complex nature of quality in ECEC requires multi-faceted policy solutions. The review framework conceptualises the linkages between process quality and five high-level policy levers that can be instrumental in building ECEC systems that foster children's daily experiences: quality standards, governance and financing; curriculum and pedagogy; workforce development; monitoring and data; and family and community engagement (Figure 1.2).

Figure 1.2. Five policy areas to support high-quality early childhood education and care

Quality beyond Regulations policy review framework

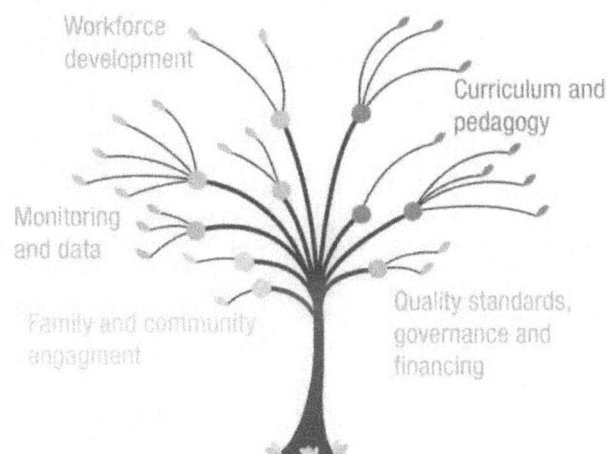

Source: OECD (2021[7]), *Starting Strong: Mapping Quality in Early Childhood Education and Care*, https://quality-ecec.oecd.org.

A specific country review of early childhood education and care in Luxembourg

As part of the *Quality beyond Regulations* policy review, this specific country policy review focuses on the quality of ECEC in Luxembourg, particularly on policies that can support process quality. Building on the five policy levers of the *Quality beyond Regulations* policy framework (Figure 1.2), the review puts a specific emphasis on aspects related to: 1) workforce development (including staff training on pedagogical practices and preparedness to support multilingualism); and 2) quality assurance and improvement (including the governance and regulatory context, and monitoring of the implementation of the national curriculum framework for non-formal ECEC). Equity and diversity are included as a cross-cutting dimension.

The scope of the review focuses on all registered, licensed or otherwise regulated ECEC settings. ECEC typically refers to all regulated settings serving children between 0 and 5 or 6 years old (see Box 1.3). However, the main focus of the review is non-formal settings, which serve children from birth until entry into the formal schooling system at age 3 or 4, as well as children up to entry in secondary schools during out-of-school time (i.e. before and after school as well as during lunch breaks and school holidays in so-called *maisons relais*). The review also discusses, to a lesser extent, ECEC within the formal sector, which begins with an optional year for children at age 3 before two years of compulsory ECEC from age 4. Furthermore, as Luxembourg is implementing an ambitious programme for multilingual education in ECEC, the country has asked for a special focus on this programme in the review.

Box 1.3. Formal and non-formal education and types of ECEC settings in Luxembourg

Luxembourg has a split system for ECEC. The two components are known as formal education and non-formal education (Figure 1.3).

Figure 1.3. Early childhood education and care settings in Luxembourg

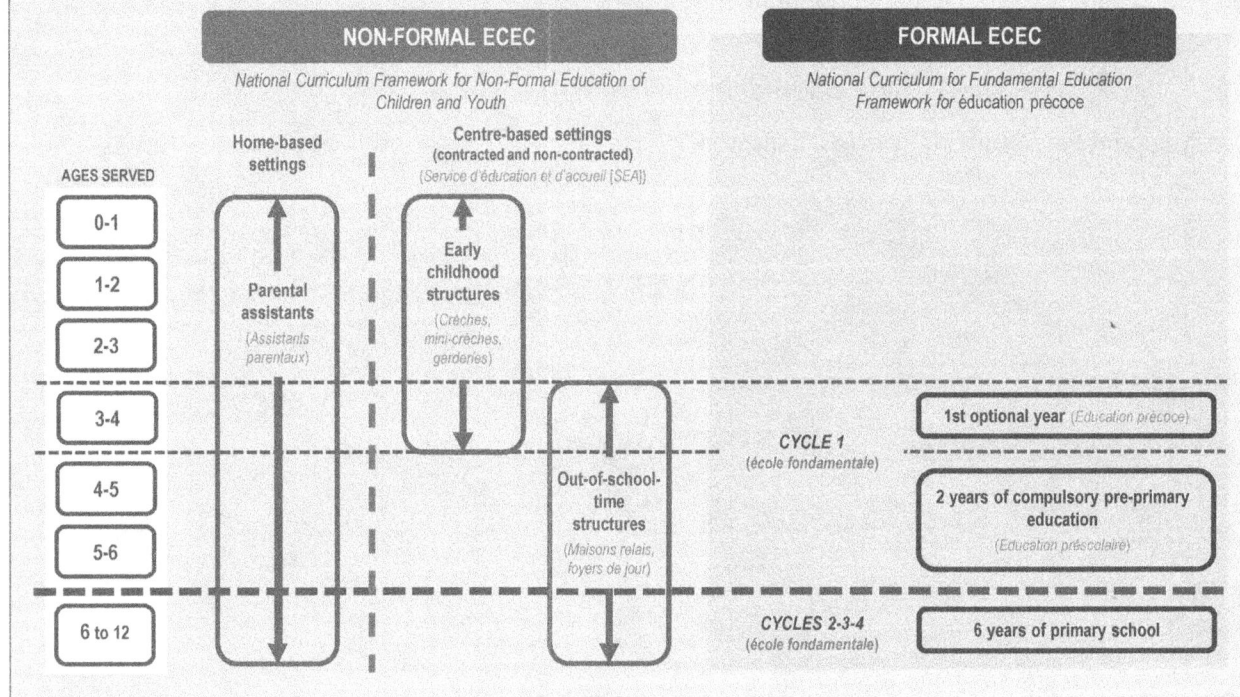

Formal education takes places in the schooling sector, beginning at age 3 with an optional year of ECEC (*éducation précoce*), followed by two compulsory years of ECEC from age 4 (*éducation préscolaire*). Together with six years of primary school, these three years of formal ECEC comprise "foundational education" (*école fondamentale*) in Luxembourg. Non-formal education encompasses ECEC for young children who are not yet enrolled in the formal education system, as well as education and care for school-age children during out-of-school hours.

This split system stems from a historic separation between elements of education and care for young children, with the services for very young children and for older children during non-school hours being viewed as primarily to support women's involvement in the labour force. However, the Law on Youth from 4 July 2008 introduced the notion of non-formal education, and since 2013, with its integration into the Ministry of Education, Children and Youth (MENJE), the non-formal sector has been officially recognised as having an educational mission.

An implementation regulation (2013) of the ASFT Act (*Loi du 8 septembre 1998 réglant les relations entre l'Etat et les organismes oeuvrant dans les domaines social, familial et thérapeutique*) regulated ECEC and specified the qualifications requirements for staff working in this sector. The Law of 24 April 2016, modifying the Law on Youth, linked the financing of ECEC with quality obligations for ECEC settings. The National Youth Service (Service national de la jeunesse; SNJ) was assigned responsibility for fostering quality in the non-formal sector, namely for monitoring process quality and the implementation of the curriculum framework for non-formal education (*Cadre de référence national sur l'éducation non formelle des enfants et des jeunes*).

In addition, Luxembourg has a long history of recognising the important role of ECEC in the formal sector, making it compulsory from age 5 in 1976 and from age 4 in 1992. Since 2009, children have been legally entitled to a place in ECEC in the formal sector from age 3.

The provision of ECEC in Luxembourg involves many types of settings. Centre-based settings in the non-formal sector are known as *services d'éducation et d'accueil* (SEA) and include ECEC for children under age 3 (e.g. crèches, mini-crèches) and for school-age children during their out-of-school time (e.g. *maisons relais*, *foyers de jour*). These different ECEC services can be offered by providers contracted by the government (*structures conventionnées*) or operate independently but are nonetheless licensed and regulated by the government (*structures non-conventionnées*). Home-based ECEC is provided by *assistants parentaux* who are regulated and work independently, hence part of the non-contracted sector only. School-based settings operate in the formal sector.

In the non-formal sector, most centre-based settings offer services either for very young children before they begin their formal education or for school-age children. For school-age children, ECEC is available in both the formal and non-formal sectors. Children can attend ECEC in the formal sector for 26 hours per week, with ECEC before and after school as well as during the lunch break in the non-formal sector. On average, children under age 3 attend centre-based ECEC for 32 hours per week. Children age 3 and over attend a combination of centre- and school-based ECEC for approximately 35 hours per week.

Home-based ECEC providers can take up to five children, but only two children under age 2. Centre-based ECEC settings must have a child-to-adult ratio not exceeding six children under age 2 per adult and eight children aged 2-4 per adult. In the first, non-compulsory year of pre-primary education in the formal sector, there is a maximum of 20 children with one teacher and one educator (e.g. assistant) (see Chapter 2). In the compulsory years of pre-primary education, there is an average of 16 children with one teacher.

The review is based on a mixed-method design and uses a combination of both quantitative and qualitative analysis, drawing on both national and international data and evidence. The review process entailed the preparation of a country background report (CBR) (SNJ, 2021[8]). This CBR consists of a self-assessment conducted by the Luxembourgish authorities following the review's conceptual framework and detailed guidelines from the OECD. The data from the CBR are a primary source of information for this publication.

The review was undertaken by an OECD-led team providing an independent analysis of ECEC policies in the country. The OECD review team comprised Stéphanie Jamet (Head of the OECD team for Early Childhood Education and Care), Victoria Liberatore (OECD), Elizabeth Shuey (OECD), Katharina Ereky-Stevens (University of Oxford) and Kathy Sylva (University of Oxford). The review team engaged in virtual conversations between May 2021 and October 2021 to collect a broad cross-section of evidence and views on ECEC policies from key stakeholder groups in Luxembourg. In addition, limited in-person meetings and site visits, given the context of the COVID-19 pandemic, took place in October 2021. Annex A provides a detailed description of the objectives and schedule of these meetings.

Semi-structured interviews were conducted with a wide range of stakeholders, including those in government departments, national agencies, inspections, training providers, non-governmental organisations, providers of ECEC services, researchers and others. The OECD review team also spoke to leaders and staff from four types of ECEC settings. Each meeting contributed to the review team's understanding of ECEC in Luxembourg and the role of different actors.

The missions were designed by the OECD in collaboration with the Luxembourgish authorities. The co-ordination of the work within Luxembourg was undertaken by the National Youth Service (Service national de la jeunesse), a public service created by law that is integrated with the Ministry of Education, Children and Youth (*Ministère de l'Éducation nationale, de l'Enfance et de la Jeunesse*).

The review was organised with the support of the European Commission (EC), which co-financed the review in the context of a broader partnership established between the OECD and the EC for the project. A representative of the EC participated as an observer in some of the review's visits (Livia Ruszthy and Géraldine Libreau). The EC was not involved in the drafting of this report, and views expressed herein can in no way be taken to reflect the official opinion of the European Union.

Structure and scope of the report

The review aims to identify strengths, challenges and policy recommendations with a particular focus in the areas of workforce development, and quality assurance and improvement. In addition to this introductory chapter, this report includes two thematic chapters on the two main areas of the review and a summary of the assessments and recommendations. The scope of the review does not directly include issues related to governance and funding of ECEC; however, as these shape the core conditions for the two main areas of analysis, they are discussed as context to the review in this chapter.

Workforce development and quality assurance and improvement are powerful policy levers that can help drive improvement in the sector. The workforce's preparation, ongoing professional development and working conditions are key to boosting staff practices, which are one of the most proximal factors to children's experiences in ECEC, together with policies around curriculum and pedagogy. The ECEC workforce in Luxembourg reflects the highly multilingual and multicultural society in which it is embedded. While this diversity can be a strength for tailoring services to the wide range of needs and preferences from families, it also poses a challenge for building a shared understanding of quality in the sector and for promoting the language skills that are foundational for young children growing up in Luxembourg. The quality assurance and improvement system is crucial to track and improve ECEC quality, ensuring successful implementation of the ambitious policies for the sector and value for investments in the early years.

The policy context of early childhood education and care in Luxembourg

Governance, funding and enrolment

Luxembourg's Ministry of Education, Children and Youth (*Ministère de l'Éducation nationale, de l'Enfance et de la Jeunesse*, MENJE) is responsible for implementing formal ECEC and guaranteeing non-formal ECEC through a licensing and service agreement process (see Box 1.3). Within MENJE, the National Youth Service (Service national de la jeunesse, SNJ) is responsible for many aspects of non-formal education, notably the development and implementation of the relevant curriculum framework (*Bildungsrahmenplan*) as well as continuing professional development for staff working in this sector. SNJ collaborates with another unit within MENJE, the Department for Children (*Direction générale du secteur de l'Enfance*) to monitor quality in non-formal ECEC settings. Responsibility for the formal ECEC sector falls across other units of MENJE but is mainly overseen by the Department for Fundamental Education (*Direction générale de l'Enseignement fondamental*), which covers both pre-primary and primary education in Luxembourg.

Participation in ECEC is widespread in Luxembourg. In 2019, approximately 61% of children under age 3 were enrolled in non-formal ECEC in Luxembourg, which is above the OECD average of 25% for participation in ISCED 0 settings among this age group. Furthermore, over 87% of 3-year-olds were enrolled in the first optional pre-primary education year (*éducation précoce*, Box 1.3) in 2017, representing strong engagement with formal ECEC in the year before compulsory schooling begins.

Luxembourg has invested in supporting access to both non-formal and formal ECEC, with a particular goal of fostering multilingualism: children ages 1-4 are legally entitled to 20 hours of free non-formal education in centre-based settings that meet requirements to provide programming in both Luxembourgish and French. From age 3, children are entitled to a place in formal ECEC through the schooling system.

Expenditure in ECEC in Luxembourg reflects this commitment to supporting access and represented 0.5% of GDP in 2018, similar to the OECD average of 0.6% (from both public and private sources). The modest investments as a percentage of GDP must be understood in the context of Luxembourg's overall strong economy, including the highest GDP per capita among OECD countries (OECD, 2022[9]). The annual expenditure per child aged 3-5 in 2018 in Luxembourg was well above the OECD average (USD 20 921 compared to USD 9 123, converted using purchasing power parity [PPP]; Figure 1.4) (OECD, 2021[3]).

ECEC services in the formal sector are offered through the schooling system, which is predominantly public. Only 11% of children ages 3-6 attend ECEC in private schools, well below the OECD average of 33% for pre-primary education (OECD, 2021[3]). In the non-formal sector, ECEC services are offered through municipalities or private providers that are either contracted by the government (*structures conventionnées*) or not contracted by the government (*structures non-conventionnées*). Contracted providers are typically non-profit organisations, whereas non-contracted providers are mostly commercial enterprises. In addition, approximately 4% of the places available in non-formal ECEC are with home-based providers (*assistants parentaux*) (Box 1.3).

As of 2019, contracted services in the non-formal sector represented approximately 74% of the centre-based ECEC and out-of-school-time places available for children ages 0-12. However, for children from birth until school entry, these contracted services represent only approximately 30% of available centre-based ECEC places. This difference means that very young children tend to be enrolled in commercial, for-profit settings, whereas school-age children are more likely to spend their out-of-school time with non-profit providers. The ECEC sector expanded dramatically in Luxembourg in the last decade, with contracted places for children more than doubling between 2009 and 2019 and non-contracted places growing even more, to more than five times their availability in 2009. The rapid expansion of ECEC settings in the last decade has placed qualified ECEC staff in high demand.

Figure 1.4. Annual expenditure per child aged 3-5 enrolled in ECEC and primary education, 2018

Public and private institutions, in USD, converted using PPPs

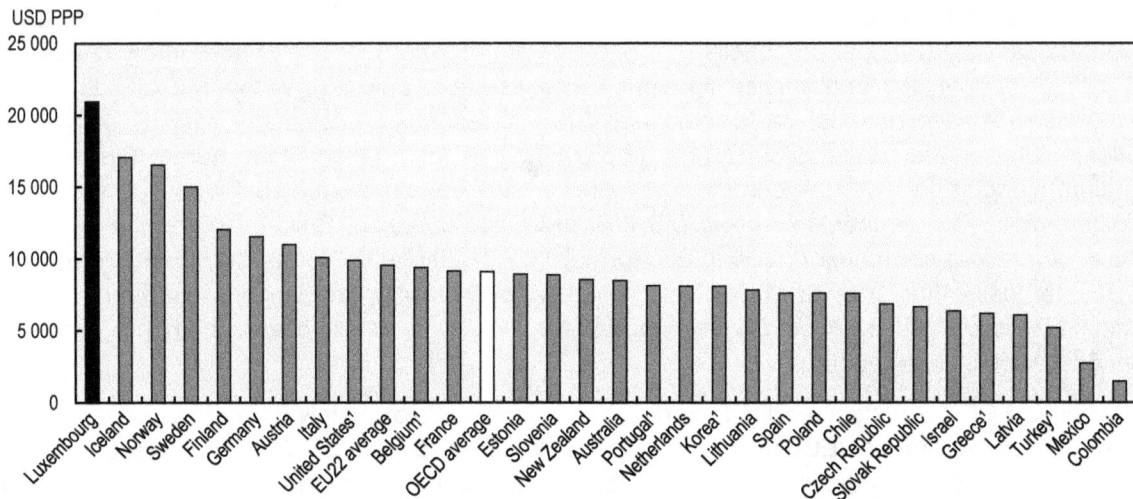

Note: Data for Luxembourg reflect only expenditures through the formal education system and do not include expenditures through the non-formal education system.
1. Expenditure excludes expenditure and enrolment in ISCED 01 programmes.
Source: OECD (2021[3]), *Education at a Glance 2021: OECD Indicators*, Table B2.3, https://dx.doi.org/10.1787/b35a14e5-en.

The growth in the non-formal education sector corresponds with the government's introduction of a subsidy funding scheme (*chèques-service accueil*, CSA) in 2009. The CSA funding is intended to increase access to high-quality ECEC and out-of-school-time programming to advance equity goals. All children ages 0-12 living in Luxembourg are entitled to benefit from the CSA, and children living in neighbouring countries can also benefit from the programme under certain conditions (e.g. a parent is employed in Luxembourg). As of 2019, almost 60% of children of this age group who reside in Luxembourg receive CSA. The amount of the CSA is tailored to family circumstances to reduce (or eliminate) the costs of ECEC for socio-economically disadvantaged households.

Nearly all ECEC providers in the non-formal sector are eligible to receive CSA funding: in 2019, all contracted ECEC settings, and all but six non-contracted settings received CSA funding. In addition, most (approximately 98%) home-based providers participate in the CSA system. Government payments through the CSA system to ECEC providers are the same regardless of whether the setting is contracted or non-contracted. It is capped at EUR 6 per hour per child (up to 60 hours per week) for centres and EUR 3.75 per hour per child for home-based settings. The widespread participation of ECEC providers in the CSA system means that families should generally be able to choose an ECEC provider that best meets their needs and goals for their children. However, centre- and home-based options are not equally distributed throughout the country, and as access to non-formal education is not an entitlement, demand for certain types of providers can exceed supply in some municipalities. Furthermore, parental fees in home-based and non-contracted centre-based settings are uncapped.

In addition to subsidising families' costs, the CSA system administers 20 hours of free ECEC to children ages 1-4 in centre-based settings as part of a programme to provide early support for multilingualism. Beginning in 2022, out-of-school time services in the non-formal sector will also be fully free to families from 7:00 a.m. to 7:00 p.m. on schooldays, underscoring the government's commitment to reducing access barriers and encouraging participation of all children in these programmes. These entitlements to free

ECEC in the non-formal education sector complement the free public-school offer (*éducation précoce* and *éducation préscolaire*) from age 3.

Costs to parents is a main barrier to ECEC participation in many countries, particularly for low-income families. But between the free and subsidised ECEC available to families, Luxembourg has some of the most affordable childcare costs for families among OECD countries (Figure 1.5). A real strength of its ECEC system is the mix of both universal and targeted entitlements. Nonetheless, ECEC in Luxembourg does have costs for families. Access to the 20 free hours of non-formal ECEC does not begin until children are age 1, leaving a gap for families between fully funded parental leave and access to some hours of free ECEC. This gap in social supports disproportionately affects lower-income families, who often also have less flexibility in their jobs.

Figure 1.5. Childcare costs for parents in OECD countries, 2019

Typical net childcare costs for two children in full-time care, in % of women's median full-time earnings, by family type and in-work earnings

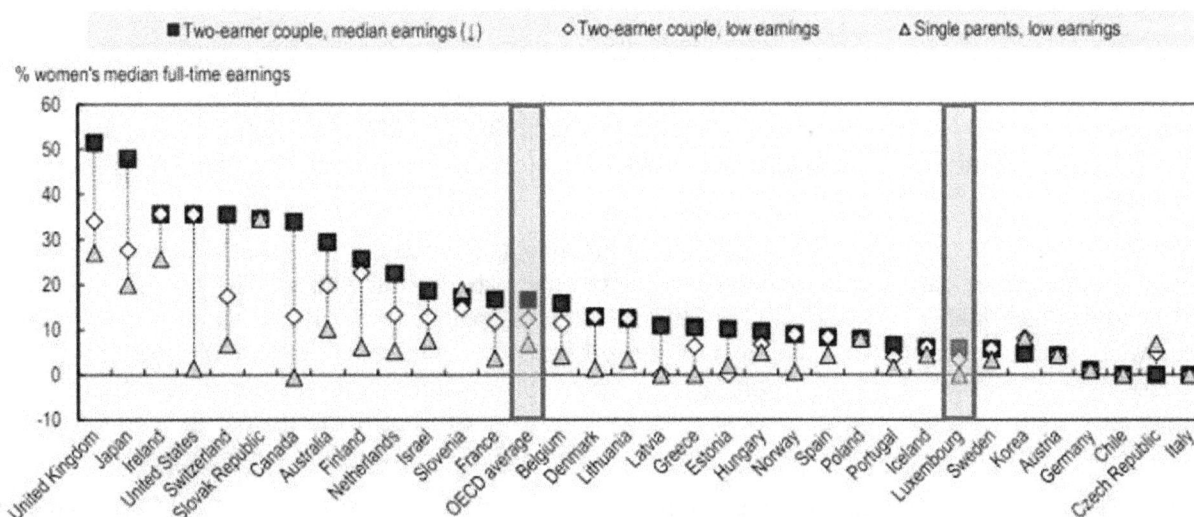

Notes: Data reflect the net cost (gross fees less childcare benefits/rebates and tax deductions, plus any resulting changes in other taxes and benefits following the use of childcare) of full-time care in a typical childcare centre for a two-child family, where both parents are in full-time employment and the children are aged 2 and 3. "Full-time" care is defined as care for at least 40 hours per week. Low earnings refer to the 20th percentile, and median earnings to the 50th percentile, of the full-time gender-specific earnings distribution. Two earners are assumed for couples, male and female. For single parents, women's earnings distribution is assumed. In countries where local authorities regulate childcare fees, childcare settings for a specific sub-national jurisdiction is assumed. For Korea, the results refer to 2018; for Chile to 2015. For Mexico, Turkey and New Zealand, information on childcare fees is not available. For Japan, data reflect the situation before the expansion of free ECEC to all children aged between 3 and 5, and to infants aged 2 and under from low-income families, in October 2019.
Source: OECD (2019[10]), *Tax and Benefit Models*, https://www.oecd.org/social/benefits-and-wages/.

Considering the high costs of ECEC for infants and the unique challenges in providing good quality group care for this age range, ECEC for very young children may still carry a high cost burden for families in Luxembourg. Luxembourg does not regulate the fees that non-contracted ECEC settings charge families, and this is the main sector offering ECEC for children under age 3. Combining information on the fees charged by non-contracted settings with the uptake of these fee-based services by diverse families would enable the government in Luxembourg to better understand the successes and limitations of the current approach to free and subsidised ECEC (see Chapter 3).

Luxembourg is a highly multicultural and multilingual society

Luxembourg is a small country, with a population of just 634 730 in 2021, approximately 6% of which is children under age 6 (Le Portail des Statistiques, 2021[11]). Yet, this number reflects the strongest population growth among European Union countries in the last decade, highlighting the role of migration in shaping the country's demographics (Eurostat, 2021[12]). Luxembourg has the highest share of a foreign-born population among OECD countries, with 47.3% of the population falling in this category (OECD, 2022[13]). In addition, the country's small geographic area facilitates cross-border workers, who numbered nearly 200 000 in 2020, from neighbouring Belgium, France and Germany. These workers are eligible to benefit from the CSA system to subsidise participation of their young children in ECEC in Luxembourg.

In addition to the migration dynamics that mean the population of Luxembourg has a myriad of language backgrounds, the country has three official languages: Luxembourgish, French and German. These languages are not restricted to certain geographic areas of the countries but rather are applied in different aspects of life and education. As such, multilingualism is a valued part of the Luxembourgish identity, and the government is committed to supporting multilingual education beginning in early childhood.

Luxembourgish is the main language of ECEC in the formal sector, yet in the 2019/20 school year, only 33.7% of students enrolled in formal education in Luxembourg spoke Luxembourgish as their main language at home (LUCET/Université du Luxembourg/SCRIPT, 2021[14]). Since 2017, multilingual initiatives in the formal and non-formal sectors have aimed to support young children's development across languages.

In the formal sector, this means including a playful initiation to French during the ECEC years, as well as recognising the many other home-languages children bring with them to school. The approach is holistic and child-centred, taking into account the needs, interests and talents of all children, in an effort to acknowledge and valorise their existing multilingual potential. The curriculum for ECEC in the formal sector includes language skills – listening, speaking and first steps towards reading and writing – that are to be developed during these early years of schooling. Minimum levels of competence are defined for children in the primary school years, when literacy education begins in earnest and is done in German.

In the non-formal sector, a new multilingual education programme was also launched in 2017, building as well on a playful initiation to languages. ECEC centres serving children aged 1-4 are obligated to implement the multilingual education programme in order to receive CSA funding. The multilingual programme aims to promote the different home languages of children but places specific emphasis on ensuring children are exposed to both French and Luxembourgish. To support this goal, at least one person with basic fluency (language level C1) in French and one in Luxembourgish must be employed. In addition, each centre must appoint a pedagogical referent (*référent(e) pédagogique pour l'éducation plurilingue*) who co-ordinates the implementation of multilingual education for the setting. A specific 30-hour training course is offered free of charge by the National Youth Service for these designated referents. In addition, all ECEC staff in the non-formal sector must have content on language development included in their ongoing professional development.

The multilingual education programme benefits from input from a scientific council, which was involved in establishing the programme and advises on its ongoing implementation. In addition, parents are viewed as key partners in this programme, and their involvement in sharing their languages and cultures in ECEC settings is a core pillar of the programme.

The government in Luxembourg recognises the importance of early childhood as a time to promote language development and begin to give all children opportunities to learn the multiple languages that will enable them to participate fully in Luxembourgish society. However, despite the strong commitment to ongoing professional development to train staff in this new multilingual programme model, the country faces a shortage of qualified personnel to fully implement the multilingual vision in non-formal ECEC. Notably, the requirement to have a fluent speaker of Luxembourgish on staff is a challenge, particularly for non-contracted settings, where wages are lower compared with contracted settings (see Chapter 2). Although centres that participate in the multilingual programme receive additional funding through the CSA system to help attract and retain the staff necessary to implement this programme, the limited supply of ECEC staff fluent in Luxembourgish needs to be addressed.

In addition to ongoing training on pedagogy and multilingualism, MENJE could consider creating incentives for qualified ECEC staff to pursue courses in Luxembourgish. For instance, regional officers who are responsible for monitoring and strengthening quality could make recommendations to settings to encourage participation in Luxembourgish courses for staff who need it. This approach could increase the number of ECEC staff with good knowledge of the Luxembourgish language, remove barriers to finding personnel with these language skills who may lack training in ECEC and target those who may be motivated to stay in their ECEC settings. Specific language training may be particularly useful for ECEC staff who work in Luxembourg but completed their qualifications to work in ECEC outside the country.

There is also a general shortage of staff with sufficient and appropriate training to successfully implement the ambitious multilingual programme. As discussed in Chapter 2, this comes from limitations of the initial training programmes staff undertake to qualify to work in the non-formal ECEC sector, as well as a diversity of training experiences related to staff coming from neighbouring countries to work in Luxembourg. The COVID-19 pandemic has contributed to a backlog of pedagogical referents seeking the basic training to fulfil their duties, although it is also recognised that trainings are needed more broadly for ECEC staff and for leaders especially, in order to fully embed the principles of multilingual education in ECEC settings (see Chapter 2). Similarly, training for the regional officers responsible for monitoring the implementation of the multilingual programme is occurring in parallel, and these officers need ongoing support to ensure their work with ECEC settings is aligned with the intent of the multilingual programme (see Chapter 3).

Non-formal education is guided by a comprehensive curriculum framework

Luxembourg is unique in its recognition of non-formal education as a continuum of services for children from birth through adolescents' transition into adulthood, guided and regulated through a unifying curriculum framework (*Cadre de référence national sur l'éducation non formelle des enfants et des jeunes*). This curriculum framework for non-formal education includes dedicated sections on ECEC for young children who are not yet enrolled in the formal education system, and for children who are simultaneously attending formal education, as well as for older youth. The curriculum framework was first introduced in 2013 before becoming compulsory in 2017. A revision of the non-formal curriculum framework published in 2021 aims to introduce more coherence between different chapters and include new ones on children's participation and rights, on the transition phases and on ethics concerning work with children. Review and renewal of the curriculum is intended to occur every three years. The next edition is expected to focus on making the text more accessible for practitioners.

Importantly, the curriculum framework for non-formal education recognises that children's learning and development is actively occurring regardless of whether they are in a school-based formal education setting. Furthermore, the designation of "non-formal" for this sector distinguishes it both from formal education, but also from informal learning: The non-formal education sector is rooted in a social pedagogical approach and guided by clear goals around children's learning, to support their overall educational needs and to foster their individual interests. The intentional ways in which staff in ECEC settings accompany children as agents of their own learning is viewed as a key mechanism for enhancing and sustaining high quality in the sector.

The curricula for formal and non-formal education are seen as complementary. The curriculum for the formal sector (*Plan d'études de l'école fondamentale*) covers both pre-primary and primary schooling, with a separate supplement for the first, non-compulsory year of formal education. The learning areas identified in the formal education curriculum are also reflected in the non-formal curriculum framework (Figure 1.6), although covered for broader age groups in the latter. One goal of this high-level alignment is to facilitate transitions for children between non-formal and formal settings, both for children's initial entry to the formal system and throughout the day as children move between formal and non-formal education.

The alignment of the formal and non-formal curriculum frameworks notwithstanding, non-formal education in Luxembourg is carefully distinguished from formal education in several ways. For example, unlike formal education, non-formal education does not have defined competences that children of different ages should achieve, and as such, non-formal education has no system of assessment for individual children's skills. This does not preclude ECEC staff from observing children's individual development, discussing with parents and documenting these learning journeys; however, the goal is to support and develop children's interests while providing opportunities for exploration across the areas described in the non-formal curriculum.

Figure 1.6. Learning areas in Luxembourg's non-formal and formal curriculum frameworks

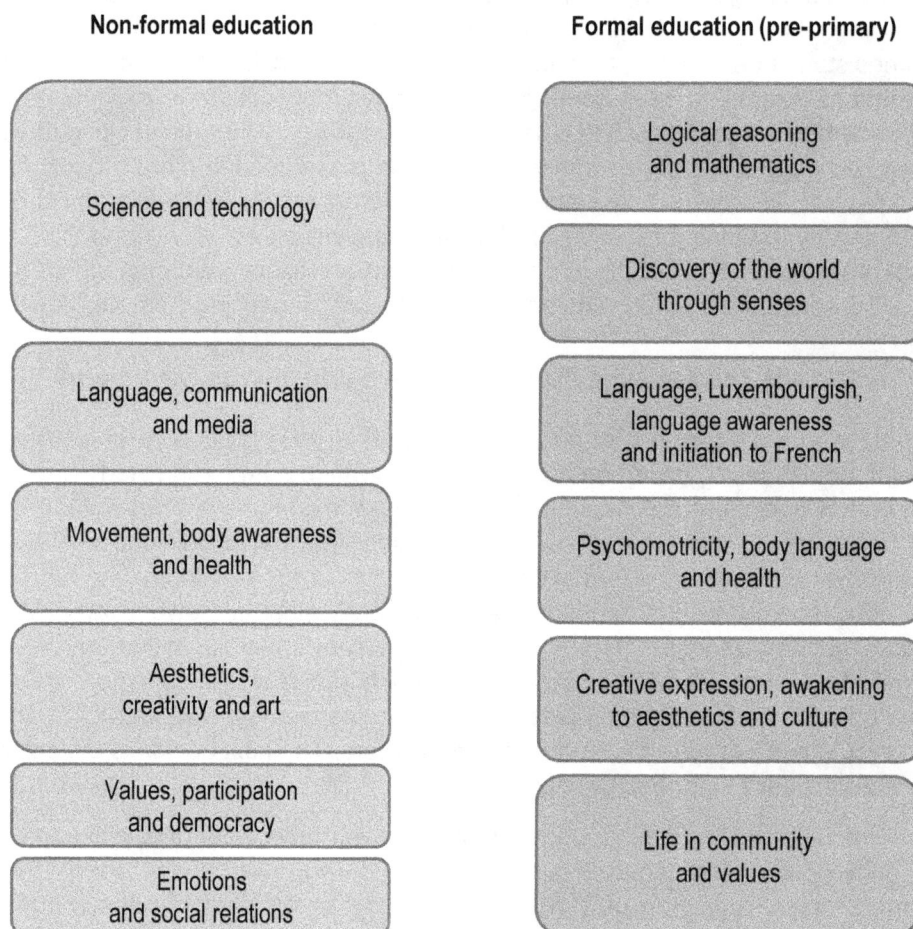

Non-formal education

- Science and technology
- Language, communication and media
- Movement, body awareness and health
- Aesthetics, creativity and art
- Values, participation and democracy
- Emotions and social relations

Formal education (pre-primary)

- Logical reasoning and mathematics
- Discovery of the world through senses
- Language, Luxembourgish, language awareness and initiation to French
- Psychomotricity, body language and health
- Creative expression, awakening to aesthetics and culture
- Life in community and values

Source: Adapted from Shuey, E. et al. (2019[15]), "Curriculum alignment and progression between early childhood education and care and primary school: A brief review and case studies", https://dx.doi.org/10.1787/d2821a65-en.

The carefully articulated curriculum framework for non-formal education, and its compulsory status for all non-formal ECEC settings in Luxembourg, including home-based providers, is a strength for building a high-quality ECEC system. The concept of process quality is embedded in the curriculum framework, with its emphasis on building relationships and learning through interactions with others and with the environment. Furthermore, the non-formal curriculum framework includes a dedicated section on working with children from birth to entry into the formal schooling system; this is another strength of Luxembourg's approach as not all countries have a curriculum framework for these first years of ECEC. Having a required curriculum framework for this stage of development recognises the foundational learning that occurs in ECEC during these years and explicitly supports children's transitions through the educational system. It also provides guidance for staff in intentionally supporting children's exploration and engagement with others and with their environments, thereby contributing to the professionalisation of this workforce.

However, the availability of staff ready to implement this framework poses a challenge. The government makes strong investments in ongoing professional development, recognising the central role on-the-job experience and continuing learning have for this workforce. Still, the curriculum framework is a complex document that requires more than a few days of professional development to master, particularly for ECEC staff with limited initial education to support this aspect of their work and with limited time to devote from their working hours (see Chapter 2).

In addition to continuing to provide strong training and professional development opportunities for ECEC staff to learn about the curriculum framework and its practical application, MENJE might consider progressively implementing requirements for ECEC centres to employ staff with higher educational qualifications and more specific knowledge of the curriculum framework for non-formal education. This role could overlap with the multilingual pedagogical referent, or with the leadership of the setting, provided that there is sufficient administrative support to allow a setting leader to engage actively and regularly in pedagogical work alongside staff. The goal of systematically including such a person at the centre level would be to improve the regular, pedagogical support for ECEC staff as they implement the non-formal curriculum framework. Eventually, this pedagogical role could be expanded to include a larger proportion of staff within each centre, effectively creating teams of lead pedagogues working alongside staff with existing, more limited, qualifications (see Chapter 2). To some extent, this model may already be in place informally in contracted ECEC settings, where salaries are higher than for non-contracted settings, thereby creating rewarding career opportunities and facilitating the retention of multilingual pedagogical referents.

For small centres that might already face difficulties in attracting and retaining a multilingual pedagogical referent, the burden of filling or creating this type of position could be prohibitive in the near term. In the short term, this problem can be addressed by encouraging centres to make use of the educational support available through the reforms to the continuous professional development system. This support is available without costs to centres and is intended to develop the educational practice of a team, to develop the educational concept or to help a team on a particular project. For centres lacking a permanent pedagogical referent or when the pedagogical referent has not yet been fully trained for their role, use of this newly available educational support should be strongly encouraged by regional officers.

The sector will need time to develop and recruit for this role, with new people entering the workforce as well as through upskilling existing ECEC staff. A move towards recognising greater and more targeted educational attainment in the ECEC workforce will require more differentiated pay scales in the non-formal sector overall, and better alignment between salaries in contracted and non-contracted settings. Eventually, this strategy could create a career pathway in the non-formal sector that could lead to lower staff turnover and increased quality for children.

Resources are uneven across the ECEC sector

Despite overall strong investment in ECEC in Luxembourg, the clear divisions in the ECEC sector (formal versus non-formal and contracted versus non-contracted) contribute to an array of services that are unevenly resourced, and therefore often of uneven quality.

Staff qualifications are a primary area of difference between the formal and non-formal education sectors in Luxembourg (see Chapter 2). In the formal sector, ECEC teachers must have a bachelor-level (ISCED

Level 6) qualification, the same level of education as their peers teaching later stages of schooling. Staff in the non-formal sector, on the other hand, are only required to have a technical qualification as part of their secondary education (i.e. ISCED Level 3), with one staff member required to have an ISCED 6 (or above) qualification in centres serving 40 children or more. In addition to the low level of qualifications required for ECEC staff in the non-formal sector, the training available in Luxembourg covers a broad range of social areas (including working with the elderly and with people with specific handicaps). This broad training can provide a good foundation for future ECEC staff to develop more specific skills on the job, but it does not necessarily suggest a strong attachment to the field of early childhood itself. These differences in human resources between formal and non-formal education are large and create different needs for ongoing training to support the conditions for high-quality ECEC. The different departments within MENJE that oversee formal and non-formal education respond to the specific needs of the teachers and staff for whom they are responsible, often leaving little room to consider the sector as a whole.

Wages in Luxembourg are high compared to neighbouring countries, reinforcing the interests of commuters who live abroad but work in Luxembourg. Nonetheless, compared to other sectors within the country, salaries for ECEC staff in the non-formal sector, and specifically in non-contracted settings, are relatively low. Staff working in contracted settings benefit from a collective pay agreement with regular increases, whereas staff working in non-contracted settings are only protected by the national minimum wage. In addition, contracted ECEC settings receive government support for 75-100% of their operating costs, including physical buildings, limiting the high overhead associated with real estate in Luxembourg. This is in addition to the fact that contracted settings receive the same level of CSA benefits per child as non-contracted settings. Contracted settings also receive funding from the government to use towards staff professional development, although the funding mechanism for professional development is changing and has now been extended to non-contracted settings (see Chapter 2 for information on reforms to this system). These government-provided financial supports for contracted settings enable them to offer the higher wages required by their workforce, thereby attracting more qualified staff (in particular those who speak Luxembourgish), leading to what is viewed by stakeholders and the monitoring system as settings with higher quality ECEC for children.

In order to compensate for the lower levels of government financing in the non-contracted sector, staff wages are generally lower, contributing to a workforce with lower qualifications or who commute from abroad and lack the language skills required by the multilingual programme and who may bring divergent views on quality in ECEC from those that are described in the curriculum framework for non-formal education. ECEC budgets in the non-contracted sector must ensure both the viability of the setting without the same financial supports received in the contracted sector, as well as some degree of profitability to encourage private providers to enter the market. These private providers are concentrated in the services available for children under age 3 or 4 (when formal education becomes available), compared to the non-profit, contracted providers who dominate the sector for out-of-school-time programmes. As highlighted by the rapid growth in the non-contracted sector following the introduction of the CSA system, the private sector is essential to the supply of ECEC in Luxembourg. Thus, the government must carefully balance requirements in the sector that could improve quality but lead to higher costs for non-contracted settings with the need to encourage private actors to enter and stay in the market.

The ongoing reforms to the professional development system aim to rebalance, to some extent, financial resources and quality across contracted and non-contracted settings, making investments more equitable across the two types of settings. With this important shift in policy, it will be essential for the government to carefully monitor implementation of the requirements for professional development across types of settings as well as related indicators of quality (see Chapter 3). The new professional development strategy can support quality improvements through the stronger investment in staff in the non-contracted sector, but it is not clear how the associated savings to private providers will be used in the system. Given the for-profit nature of many non-contracted providers, this additional government investment may serve to increase profitability rather than being passed along to families in the form of lower prices for ECEC or otherwise reinvested in quality improvement strategies to benefit children. With the need for private sector ECEC, government support for profitability is not inherently problematic, provided that strong mechanisms are in place to simultaneously ensure high quality. The government recognises these issues around ECEC supply and profitability and is implementing new monitoring strategies in an effort to better track and improve quality throughout the non-formal sector (see Chapter 3).

With system reforms ongoing and in multiple areas, it will also be important for Luxembourg to look carefully at the real costs of implementing high-quality ECEC that is consistent with the regulations and vision for this sector. Conducting research to better understand the costs to settings (both contracted and non-contracted) of providing high-quality ECEC will inform the best longer-term strategies for efficiently allocating the government's strong investments in ECEC across different types of providers. Such a review could inform the appropriateness of the divergent wages and working conditions in contracted and non-contracted settings, with a goal of eventually aligning wages more with qualifications than with the type of setting in which staff work. As implementation of new policies begins, in the near term, it would also be beneficial for the government to reflect on and articulate the expected outcomes of strategies to enhance quality in non-contracted settings in particular. This type of exercise can be useful for guiding the monitoring of policy implementation and for setting clear expectations for the field.

Another area where attention to the balance of government investment is needed is for home-based providers. Although operating costs are lower for home-based compared with centre-based ECEC, home-based providers in Luxembourg currently receive little per child from the CSA system compared with centre-based providers. The inclusion of home-based providers in the quality assurance and improvement system for the non-formal sector is a strength of the Luxembourgish ECEC system that can be complemented by strategic investments in this workforce (see Chapter 2).

Equity in ECEC is a priority for Luxembourg, but it is not currently measured

Ensuring that all types of ECEC are of high quality is foundational for building equity for children. When quality is lower in some parts of the system, disadvantages can accumulate unevenly, limiting the potential of ECEC to support learning, development and well-being for all children. Moreover, suboptimal quality can disincentivise participation in ECEC, potentially limiting valuable opportunities for young children. Luxembourg has invested heavily in supporting equitable access to ECEC through free and subsidised offerings available to all families; however, the government lacks clear information about families who do not take up these ECEC benefits and about the quality and types of settings that are accessed by children with diverse characteristics. Without systematic monitoring of whom the supports for accessing ECEC are reaching and how variations in the quality of ECEC are distributed across the population of children in Luxembourg, it is not clear if the investments are sufficiently targeted to enhance equity (see Chapter 3).

In general, children from socio-economically disadvantaged families are less likely than their more advantaged peers to participate in ECEC (OECD, 2017[16]). This difference in ECEC access compounds with other sources of family, neighbourhood and societal disadvantage, creating gaps between children of different backgrounds that widen as they advance through school (OECD, 2017[17]). Among students who participated in the Programme for International Student Assessment (PISA) in 2018, the vast majority reported having attended ECEC, and the typical number of years of participation increased in most countries between PISA 2015 and PISA 2018 (OECD, 2020[18]). However, gaps in ECEC participation contribute to differences in later educational outcomes, as seen in the disparities in reading scores for students who had attended several years of pre-primary education compared with those who had little exposure to pre-primary education (Figure 1.7). These gaps are partially explained by students' and schools' socio-economic profiles. In Luxembourg, the differences in reading performance between students who participated more in pre-primary education and those who did not are similar to the OECD average, with a clear advantage for students who had experience in pre-primary education.

These findings from PISA provide valuable insight into the links between academic performance in adolescence and participation in ECEC in a comparable manner across countries. However, students participating in PISA in 2018 attended ECEC settings more than a decade ago. The landscape of ECEC services has shifted in Luxembourg in the intervening time. In addition, PISA findings rely on students' memories of their ECEC participation. Thus, although the PISA data are an important indicator of how ECEC is associated with later stages of education systems internationally, findings must be interpreted with these caveats in mind. This highlights the importance of examining questions of equity and access with an approach that is more timely and tailored to Luxembourg's specific context.

Figure 1.7. Gaps in reading performance by the number of years in pre-primary education, 2018

Difference in the PISA reading scores of 15-year-old students who had attended pre-primary education for three years or more compared with students who had not attended or had attended for less than a year

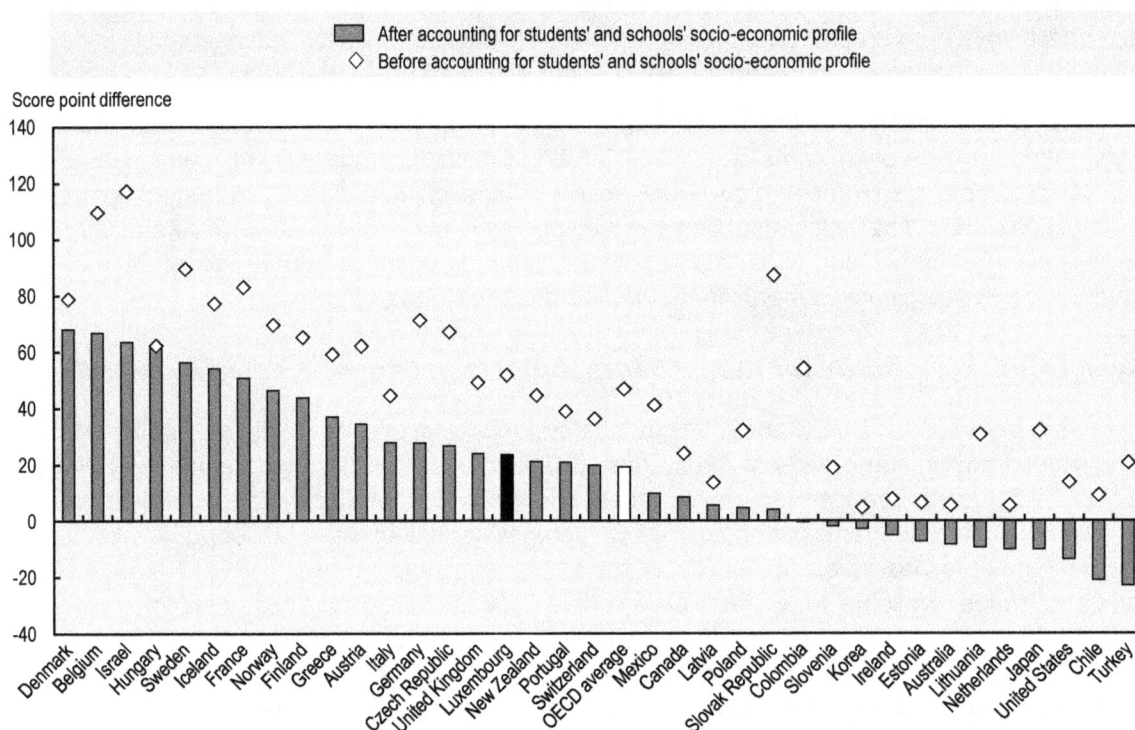

Notes: The socio-economic profile is measured by the PISA index of economic, social and cultural status (ESCS). Countries are ranked in descending order of the score point difference between students who had attended pre-primary education for three years or more and students who had not attended or had attended for less than a year.
Source: OECD (2020[18]), *PISA 2018 Results (Volume V): Effective Policies, Successful Schools*, https://dx.doi.org/10.1787/ca768d40-en.

Data from Luxembourg's national standardised testing programme covering the period 2014 to 2020 show that upon entry to primary school, children from socio-economically disadvantaged backgrounds have lower performance in Luxembourgish listening comprehension, early literacy and mathematics than their more advantaged peers (Figure 1.8). Children's home language also plays a role, with children who speak Luxembourgish or German at home performing better on these early assessments than other language groups. These differences are found despite two years of compulsory pre-primary education and could therefore be investigated by looking at the characteristics of pre-primary and non-formal education settings attended by children from different family backgrounds (see Chapter 3).

The diversity of families and children participating in ECEC is immense in Luxembourg, most evidently in relation to children's language backgrounds, but also in relation to parent values and expectations of ECEC. While language barriers, knowledge of procedures, or differences in values and beliefs can create barriers to participation (Eurofound, 2012[19]), these factors can also lead families with different background characteristics to choose or find access to different types of ECEC providers. This can cause a division between different types of providers and risk of segregation across ECEC services. Segregation can impact the degree of social mix that has been found to be beneficial to children's development, and it can create challenges for providers who serve those children and families with more disadvantages or needs (de Haan et al., 2013[20]; Early et al., 2010[21]; Kuger and Kloczniok, 2008[22]).

Figure 1.8. Gaps in early academic performance at primary school entry among students in Luxembourg, 2020

Difference in standardised test scores by family socio-economic background

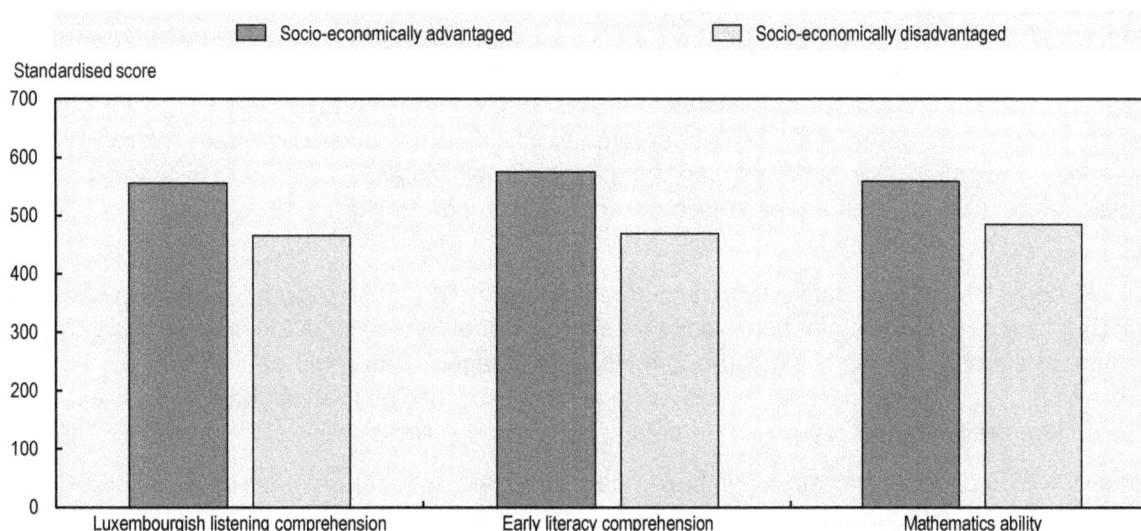

Source: LUCET (2022[23]), *EpStan Dashboard*, dashboard.epstan.lu (accessed on 10 January 2022).

Some OECD countries have designed specific financial measures to enable ECEC settings to offer good quality to groups of children with diverse needs, and to offer specific support for children with additional needs, especially for children from socio-economically disadvantaged homes, who are at risk for social exclusion. These measures are often translated into subsidies or lump sums paid to settings if they meet specific conditions or run particular educational programmes. For example, in England (United Kingdom), depending on a child's family circumstances, such as their income or whether a child is in foster care, a centre can receive additional yearly funding for each child who qualifies (Early Years Pupil Premium, EYPP). In addition, disability access funding is available to providers to help them provide appropriately tailored education and support.

Similarly, in Ireland, the Access and Inclusion Model (AIM) has been established to create a more inclusive environment in ECEC settings, providing different levels of universal and targeted support for children in response to children's needs and the specific preschool context. Support under AIM includes advice and mentoring from specialists, specialised equipment and funding for additional assistance where needed. This programme is a child-centred model designed to enable full participation in ECEC for children with special needs or disabilities, and builds on the Irish Diversity, Equality and Inclusion Charter and Guidelines for ECEC (DCYA, 2016[24]).

Identifying young children with special education needs is challenging in early childhood, but awareness of the signs that children could benefit from additional supports and early intervention from professionals can help families and ECEC staff identify individualised strategies for promoting children's development, learning and well-being. MENJE already has a Department on Inclusion (*Direction générale de l'inclusion*) that can be leveraged to support efforts to identify and support young children with special education needs. An inclusion programme targeting professionals in the non-formal sector (Incluso) is in place. However, the available funding through existing inclusion initiatives can be made more visible to ECEC settings and providers of professional development and regional officers, who are well-positioned to help identify settings where additional inclusion resources would be merited. Similarly, the specialist services that schools in the formal sector receive to collaborate with teachers and assist children with specific needs in the classroom through the policy initiative "a school for every child" (*une école pour tous*) would benefit non-formal ECEC settings as well.

Importantly, measures to support ECEC settings can exist alongside measures for extended free access that are provided directly to families, like those that exist in Luxembourg through the CSA system. As Luxembourg works to fully implement new policies around staff professional development and quality assurance and improvement, the government can consider prioritising the roll-out of these programmes in settings serving larger numbers of children from socio-economically disadvantaged and language minority backgrounds. Additional supports for the implementation of programming to support key policy goals, such as the multilingual programme, can also be targeted to ECEC settings serving more children from these demographic groups. These supports can be financial; for instance, designated funding to recruit pedagogical referents, as well as more tailored specialist supports like those available through AIM in Ireland.

In addition, home-based providers are not included in the multilingual programme. Attention is needed to ensure that children enrolled in home-based settings nonetheless have access to aspects of this programme to support their early exposure to multiple languages. This could be accomplished by having home-based providers participate in networks with centres or agencies that can offer regular experiences for children that are led by pedagogical referents or other specialised staff.

As well as creating or prioritising supports, Luxembourg can take steps to enhance equity in ECEC through increased transparency, public outreach and engagement with a wider range of stakeholders. Although these activities are already a part of the non-formal education sector to some extent, more can be done to encourage and formalise them, as well as to learn from policies in the formal education sector. Ongoing efforts to educate teachers in the formal sector about the objectives and content of the curriculum framework for non-formal education are an important component of this outreach and should be bolstered to help create bidirectional co-operation between the formal and non-formal sectors.

Notably, SNJ develops materials targeted to parents to help them understand the curriculum framework for non-formal education. These efforts are essential to helping diverse families understand the opportunities available for their children in the non-formal sector. Moving forward, SNJ can more actively and deliberately engage families in the process of creating these resources to ensure they effectively reach their target audience. Along these lines, parents and children can be more involved in future revisions to the curriculum frameworks applicable to ECEC. Luxembourg consults a relatively low number of stakeholders in these processes than many other OECD countries (OECD, 2021[6]).

Engagement with families should not be limited to those whose children already participate in the non-formal sector but must also include parents who are not yet engaged with this system or may not be seeking childcare. Families need to understand that non-formal education is distinct from formal education but that the non-formal sector nonetheless has clear educational objectives and can provide valuable opportunities for young children regardless of parents' employment status and need for childcare. Luxembourg may wish to look at strategies to support stronger parental engagement and involvement in non-formal ECEC by creating clear expectations for the sector to prioritise this dimension of quality.

Opportunities for parents to participate alongside children in ECEC centre activities can create a two-generational approach to supporting the public service mission of ECEC in Luxembourg, which is to integrate children into community life and to prepare them for Luxembourg society and school (MENJE, 2018[25]). An ECEC offer that allows for strong parental involvement can also appeal to families who may otherwise opt to care for children solely at home. The non-formal sector could also learn from strategies in the formal sector that are used to involve parents in governance and oversight; the anticipated creation of a nationally representative parent authority for non-formal education will help in this regard.

Luxembourg has an ambitious policy agenda

Non-formal education in Luxembourg has experienced rapid growth and change in recent years. Overall, the expansion of this sector reflects thoughtful investment and Luxembourg's strong commitment to providing high-quality ECEC for all children. With the integration of SNJ and the Department for Children into MENJE in 2013, the country formally recognised ECEC and out-of-school time programming as core components of education rather than simply work supports for parents. The curriculum framework for non-formal education is an ambitious vision for the field that is a driver of ongoing policy reforms around workforce development and quality assurance and improvement.

The new policies and ongoing reforms for ECEC in Luxembourg could benefit from stronger collaboration, both at the level of governance and on the ground in ECEC settings, between the formal and non-formal sectors. Within MENJE, responsibilities for different aspects of ECEC are divided across several departments. For the non-formal sector, SNJ and the Department for Children have primary responsibility, whereas the Department for Fundamental Education has primary responsibility for ECEC in the formal sector. Additional departments within the Ministry (e.g. the Service for Co-ordination of Research and Innovation in Pedagogy and Technologies [SCRIPT], the Department for Professional Development) have cross-cutting missions relevant to both sectors. Strong communication between these different departments is essential to efficiently capitalise on Luxembourg's investments in education overall and in ECEC specifically.

With the rapid pace of reforms and changes in the non-formal sector, intentional efforts are needed to keep all relevant actors moving forward together. As discussed in Chapter 3, this is especially relevant for SNJ and the Department for Children with regard to building and implementing a coherent quality assurance and improvement system. However, stronger collaboration should also be a priority between departments overseeing the formal and non-formal sectors as well. Building a greater understanding between these departments is an important step towards fully integrating the educational mission of the non-formal sector in Luxembourg's education system.

Having strong communication within the government will also help to strengthen the alignment of goals and practices for ECEC providers in the formal and non-formal sectors. The alignment of the curriculum frameworks for the two sectors underscores the intention for these different ECEC settings to work together and complement one another. In practice, however, the divergent contexts of formal and non-formal ECEC, including of staff and teacher training profiles, the approaches to quality assurance and improvement and the goals and expectations for the two sectors, can create steep challenges for co-ordination. Requirements and incentives for the two sectors to work together must be bidirectional: currently, while the two sectors are required to identify strategies to engage with one another, there is a feeling in the non-formal sector that this is not fully reciprocal. The organisation of ECEC in Luxembourg, with many children moving between the formal and non-formal sectors daily or even multiple times throughout the day, requires careful attention to the shared responsibility of supporting children in these transitions.

Strong collaboration and cohesion between the formal and non-formal ECEC sectors can support the distinct objectives and roles of the two types of programming, both of which put children at the centre. The reform currently underway to expand access to non-formal education for school-age children by eliminating costs to parents and reducing administrative procedures may encourage even more children to benefit from the unique educational experiences offered in this sector. Whether serving an expanded group of children or simply improving conditions for families already participating in both sectors, implementing this policy change offers a meaningful opportunity to simultaneously examine and improve the alignment of opportunities throughout the system from the perspective of children and families.

References

DCYA (2016), *Diverslty, Equality and Incluslon Charter and Guidelines for Early Childhood*, Departement of Children and Youth Affairs, Ireland. [24]

de Haan, A. et al. (2013), "Targeted versus mixed preschools and kindergartens: Effects of class composition and teacher-managed activities on disadvantaged children's emergent academic skills", *School Effectiveness and School Improvement*, Vol. 24/2, pp. 177-194, http://dx.doi.org/10.1080/09243453.2012.749792. [20]

Early, D. et al. (2010), "How do pre-kindergartners spend their time? Gender, ethnicity, and income as predictors of experiences in pre-kindergarten classrooms", *Early Childhood Research Quarterly*, Vol. 25, pp. 177-193, http://dx.doi.org/10.1016/j.ecresq.2009.10.003. [21]

Eurofound (2012), *Quality of Life in Europe: Impacts of the Crisis*, Publications Office of the European Union, https://www.eurofound.europa.eu/publications/report/2012/quality-of-life-social-policies/quality-of-life-in-europe-impacts-of-the-crisis. [19]

Eurostat (2021), *Population on 1 January*, https://ec.europa.eu/eurostat/databrowser/view/tps00001/default/table?lang=en (accessed on 6 December 2021). [12]

Kuger, S. and K. Kloczniok (2008), *Prozessqualität im Kindergarten, Konzept, Umsetzung und Befunde*, http://dx.doi.org/10.1007/978-3-531-91452-7_11. [22]

Le Portail des Statistiques (2021), *Population by age and sex as of January 1*, Grand-Duché de Luxembourg, https://statistiques.public.lu/stat/TableViewer/tableView.aspx?ReportId=12854&IF_Language=fra&MainTheme=2&FldrName=1 (accessed on 6 December 2021). [11]

LUCET (2022), *EpStan Dashboard*, Luxembourg Centre for Educational Testing, http://dashboard.epstan.lu (accessed on 10 January 2022). [23]

LUCET/Université du Luxembourg/SCRIPT (2021), *Rapport national sur l'éducation au Luxembourg 2021*, Luxembourg Centre for Educational Testing, Université du Luxembourg et Service de Coordination de la Recherche et de l'Innovation pédagogiques et technologiques, http://dx.doi.org/10.48746/bb2021lu-fr-digipub. [14]

Melhuish, E. et al. (2015), "A review of research on the effects of early childhood education and care (ECEC) upon child development. WP4.1 Curriculum and quality analysis impact review", CARE, https://ecec-care.org/fileadmin/careproject/Publications/reports/CARE_WP4_D4_1_review_of_effects_of_ecec.pdf. [2]

MENJE (2018), *Staark Kanner – Enfance*, Ministère de l'Éducation nationale, de l'Enfance et de la Jeunesse du Grand-Duché de Luxembourg, http://www.men.public.lu/fr/enfance/index.html. [25]

OECD (2022), *Foreign-born population* (indicator), https://dx.doi.org/10.1787/5a368e1b-en (accessed on 21 January 2022). [13]

OECD (2022), *Gross domestic product (GDP)* (indicator), https://dx.doi.org/10.1787/dc2f7aec-en (accessed on 21 January 2022). [9]

OECD (2021), *Education at a Glance 2021: OECD Indicators*, OECD Publishing, Paris, https://dx.doi.org/10.1787/b35a14e5-en. [3]

OECD (2021), *Starting Strong VI: Supporting Meaningful Interactions in Early Childhood Education and Care*, Starting Strong, OECD Publishing, Paris, https://dx.doi.org/10.1787/f47a06ae-en. [6]

OECD (2021), *Starting Strong: Mapping Quality in Early Childhood Education and Care*, OECD, Paris, https://quality-ecec.oecd.org. [7]

OECD (2021), *Using Digital Technologies for Early Education during COVID-19: OECD Report for the G20 2020 Education Working Group*, OECD Publishing, Paris, https://dx.doi.org/10.1787/fe8d68ad-en. [5]

OECD (2020), *Education at a Glance 2020: OECD Indicators*, OECD Publishing, Paris, https://dx.doi.org/10.1787/69096873-en. [4]

OECD (2020), "Is Childcare Affordable?", Policy Brief on Employment, Labour and Social Affairs, OECD, Paris, http://oe.cd/childcare-brief-202. [26]

OECD (2020), *PISA 2018 Results (Volume V): Effective Policies, Successful Schools*, PISA, OECD Publishing, Paris, https://dx.doi.org/10.1787/ca768d40-en. [18]

OECD (2019), *Tax and Benefit Models*, OECD, Paris, https://www.oecd.org/social/benefits-and-wages/. [10]

OECD (2018), *Engaging Young Children: Lessons from Research about Quality in Early Childhood Education and Care*, Starting Strong, OECD Publishing, Paris, https://dx.doi.org/10.1787/9789264085145-en. [1]

OECD (2017), *Educational Opportunity for All: Overcoming Inequality throughout the Life Course*, Educational Research and Innovation, OECD Publishing, Paris, https://dx.doi.org/10.1787/9789264287457-en. [17]

OECD (2017), *Starting Strong 2017: Key OECD Indicators on Early Childhood Education and Care*, Starting Strong, OECD Publishing, Paris, https://dx.doi.org/10.1787/9789264276116-en. [16]

Shuey, E. et al. (2019), "Curriculum alignment and progression between early childhood education and care and primary school: A brief review and case studies", *OECD Education Working Papers*, No. 193, OECD Publishing, Paris, https://dx.doi.org/10.1787/d2821a65-en. [15]

SNJ (2021), *Quality beyond Regulation in Early Childhood Education and Care (ECEC): Country Background Report of Luxembourg*, Service national de la jeunesse, https://www.oecd.org/education/school/StartingStrongVI-CBR-Luxembourg.pdf. [8]

2 The development of the early childhood education and care workforce in Luxembourg

This chapter considers how to build and retain an Early Childhood Education and Care (ECEC) workforce to best support quality, particularly in the non-formal sector. This includes ways to strengthen workforce preparedness, professional development, and working conditions and wages.

Introduction

Early childhood education and care (ECEC) staff are fundamental in supporting quality in ECEC systems. ECEC staff can profoundly shape children's everyday interactions, which are likely to influence their development, learning and well-being (OECD, 2021[1]; 2018[2]).

Luxembourg has made important efforts in further professionalising its ECEC workforce in the past ten years, particularly in the non-formal sector. Qualifications requirements for staff working in this sector were introduced in 2013 (see Box 1.3). In 2016, the National Youth Service (*Service national de la jeunesse*, SNJ) was assigned responsibility for fostering quality in the non-formal sector. Since then, significant investments have been made to foster quality in the non-formal sector, including increased funding to raise the quality of staff training. SNJ was also recently assigned responsibility for continuous professional development for ECEC staff. Moreover, the Ministry of Education, Children and Youth (*Ministère de l'Éducation nationale, de l'Enfance et de la Jeunesse*, MENJE) and SNJ conducted a review of the curriculum framework for non-formal education. At the time of writing, SNJ was conducting an integral reform of the continuous professional development system, which aims to expand access, make the offer free of charge for settings and improve the quality of provision.

This chapter considers Luxembourg's main strengths and challenges in building and retaining an ECEC workforce that can best support quality, particularly in the non-formal sector. It also makes recommendations to inform discussions on ongoing and future policy developments, as summarised in Box 2.1. In line with the framework of the *Quality beyond Regulations* project (OECD, 2021[1]), the discussion focuses on the following four aspects of workforce development:

1. policies to improve the skills and preparedness of ECEC professionals to work with children by strengthening initial education and training for ECEC staff and setting qualification requirements for different types of roles

2. policies to make sure ECEC staff and leaders are well prepared to foster enriching interactions through broad training that includes quality work-based learning and is well aligned with the curriculum framework

3. strategies for the continuous professional development that support the engagement of ECEC staff and leaders in a range of learning opportunities, through time and funding, matching their needs at different career stages

4. policies to ensure that staff working conditions, salaries, and employment contracts align with staff qualifications and roles.

Box 2.1. Policy recommendations

Initial preparation and training

- Strengthen the integration of the national ECEC curriculum frameworks in initial education programmes. Ensure that the *Lycée technique pour professions éducatives et sociales* (LTPES) programme (ISCED Level 3) includes the principles of the curriculum framework for non-formal education in its modules on pedagogies. Ensure that the bachelor's degrees (ISCED Level 6) in educational sciences and in social and educational sciences cover the ECEC curriculum frameworks for both formal and non-formal education.

- Explore the possibility of developing ECEC-specific initial education programmes that provide qualifications at various levels of education. Consider the possibility of introducing specialisation in ECEC in the LTPES programme or to add additional years specialised in ECEC, leading to a higher qualification (e.g. ISCED 4). Consider the possibility to develop an ISCED 5 qualification specialised in ECEC. Specialised programmes could allow existing staff to upgrade from an ISCED 3 to higher levels of qualification.

- If new qualification programmes above the ISCED 3 level and with an ECEC focus are developed as recommended, gradually recognise the roles of staff with higher pedagogical responsibilities through higher qualification requirements and wages aligned with this role. Their role could overlap with the multilingual pedagogical referent or the leader of the setting. It would need to be implemented uniformly in the non-formal sector (see Chapter 1).

- If plans to create a one-year vocational training diploma (ISCED 3) to prepare staff for working in non-formal education settings focusing on ECEC are pursued, identify options for existing staff to access to the programme, particularly those working in home-based settings and unqualified staff. Ensure that the programme's content corresponds to both the priorities of the sector and staff training needs, for instance, by taking into account the results from the monitoring of the sector done by regional officers.

- Ensure that all students who aim to work in ECEC receive enough relevant practical experience (including in non-formal education settings) during their initial education.

- Make efforts to increase the capacity of initial education institutions. This may include working with foreign universities to attract qualified teachers, and implementing hybrid training models, with both in-person and online modules.

- In consultation with experts and the ECEC sector, define long-term quality standards and monitoring frameworks for initial education programmes, including on alignment with national curricula and pedagogies for ECEC and inclusion of practical experience and mentoring.

Continuous professional development

As the reform of the continuous professional development system in the non-formal sector is implemented in 2022:

- Ensure that the reimbursement of the cost of continuous professional development for all types of settings and staff helps reduce the gap in staff preparedness between the contracted and non-contracted sectors.

- In line with the objectives of the reform, ensure that the offer of continuous professional development responds to staff training needs. It needs also to increase the training offer on curriculum framework implementation, inclusion and multilingual education. In particular, ensure availability of continuous professional development targeted to unqualified staff.

- In line with the objectives of the reform, develop strategies to support the professional development of leaders. These could include: coaching, mentoring, and a sufficient offer of trainings on management practices; implementing curriculum frameworks; supporting staff in their pedagogical work; fostering self-reflection on quality improvement in their settings; and engaging with parents, communities and the formal education sector.

- Ensure that the reform leads to the provision of training in a diversity of languages and through alternative professional development formats, including mentoring, coaching and induction programmes, in addition to training courses.

- Implement the recently agreed standards for trainers in terms of qualifications and background, as well as the quality standards on training content, and ensure that effective mechanisms for monitoring the quality of professional development provision are in place.

- Implement strategies to recruit qualified trainers with good knowledge of the national curriculum framework for non-formal education and trainers who can deliver the courses in French. For this, support co-operation with the initial education sector.

- Design mechanisms to raise staff qualifications through continuous professional development. Define paths for working staff to gain certifications through training, for instance, by developing modules of continuous professional development and work-based learning that can be incorporated in a formal qualification programme.

Staff preparedness to implement curriculum frameworks

- Continue the process of review of the curriculum framework for non-formal education, working towards a version that is simpler for staff to understand.

- Implement plans to increase the offer on trainings on multilingualism provided by SNJ, including strategies to use blended learning formats, and hire experts to provide the trainings. Provide further guidance to pedagogical referents (*référents pédagogiques*) for multilingual programmes in ECEC on how to transmit the vision and knowledge on multilingualism to the rest of staff in their settings.

- Continue to foster co-operation and formal communication within SNJ to inform the implementation of the multilingual programme.

- Prepare staff on how to communicate to parents the vision of non-formal education, the pedagogies used in the setting and the important educational work they conduct.

- Ensure that staff and teachers in both non-formal and formal ECEC are trained on the importance of continuity of children's experience across levels.

Working conditions

- Review the funding and monitoring systems to support an alignment of wages with qualifications and roles. Ensure that staff with similar profiles have similar wages in contracted and non-contracted settings within the non-formal sector (see Chapters 1 and 3).

- Facilitate employment under full-time contracts for less qualified staff (e.g. ISCED 3 qualification) by exploring further possibilities to allow them to work in both non-formal and formal education settings for children aged 3-4 (*maisons relais* and *education précoce*).

- Continue discussions in the sector on changing the status of home-based providers to improve their working conditions and the quality of their services.

The professionalisation of the workforce

Context

As studies from different national contexts and for different types of provision suggest, highly qualified staff tend to be better able to sustain enriching and stimulating interactions with children (Manning et al., 2017[3]; Lin and Magnusson, 2018[4]).

Luxembourg has made important efforts in the last decade to professionalise its ECEC workforce by strengthening the quality of ECEC staff education and training, introducing legal requirements on minimum qualifications to work in the non-formal education sector and supporting participation in continuous professional development.

The implementation regulation (2013) of the ASFT Act (*Loi du 8 septembre 1998 réglant les relations entre l'Etat et les organismes oeuvrant dans les domaines social, familial et thérapeutique*) specified the qualifications requirements for staff working in non-formal ECEC. Regulations require settings serving children under age 4 to have a minimum of 60% of staff who hold at least an International Standard Classification of Education (ISCED) Level 3 qualification in the social or educational field (*éducateur diplômé*); a maximum of 30% of staff with either lower qualifications than ISCED 3 (*auxiliaire de vie*) or other qualifications not directly related to the social or educational field; and no more than 10% of staff with no qualifications. In settings with a capacity greater than or equal to 40 children, at least one of the staff members must have a bachelor's or master's level qualification (ISCED 6 or above) in the psychosocial, pedagogical or socio-educational field. In settings for children above age 4, the required percentages are 50%, 40% and 10% in the respective categories. Within the non-formal sector, the same regulations apply to all types of settings, both contracted (*conventionné*) and non-contracted (*non-conventionné*).

While there are no available data on the qualifications of the ECEC workforce in Luxembourg, these requirements suggest that the level of qualification of ECEC staff working with the youngest children is relatively low. As a point of comparison, in Germany and Norway (countries that have also prioritised ECEC), 70-80% of ECEC staff working with children under the age of 3 have at least an ISCED 4 diploma (post-secondary non-tertiary), and 50-70% have at least an ISCED 6 diploma (bachelor's degree) (Figure 2.1).

Figure 2.1. Educational attainment of staff and content of initial training in selected countries, 2018

Staff reports of their highest level of education and whether they received training specifically to work with children

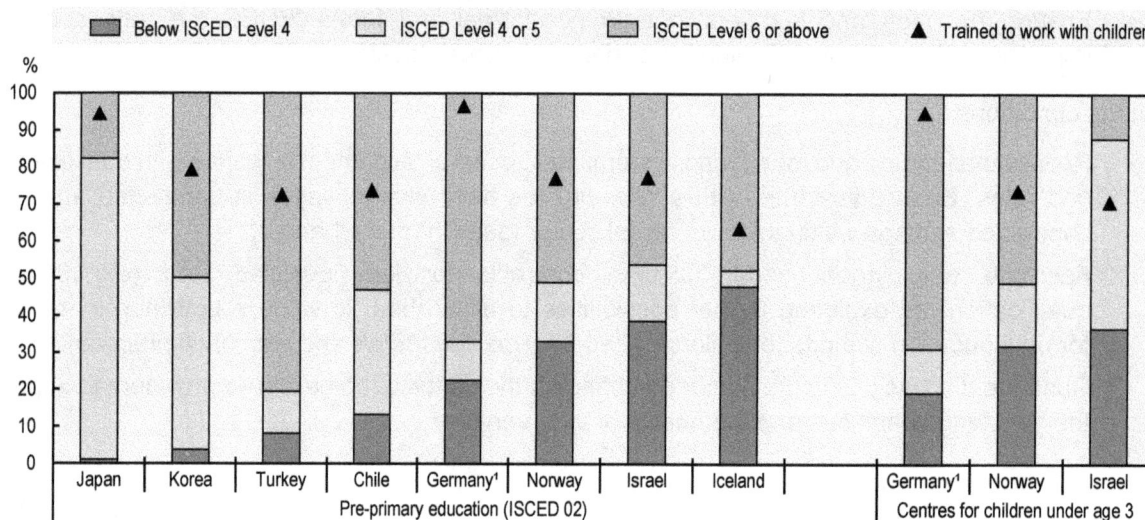

Note:
1. Estimates for sub-groups and estimated differences between sub-groups should be interpreted with care.
Respondents in the "Below ISCED Level 4" group are those whose highest education is at a secondary level or below. Respondents in the "ISCED Level 4 or 5" group are those whose highest education is beyond secondary schooling but less than a bachelor's degree (or equivalent), including post-secondary, non-tertiary education (generally vocationally oriented) and short-cycle tertiary education. Respondents in the "ISCED Level 6 or above" group are those whose highest education is at the level of a bachelor's degree or equivalent or higher.
Source: OECD (2019[5]), *Providing Quality Early Childhood Education and Care: Results from the Starting Strong Survey 2018*, https://doi.org/10.1787/301005d1-en.

Settings registered within the subsidy funding scheme (*chèques-service accueil*, CSA) that serve children aged 0 to 4 are also requested to implement the multilingual education programme and comply with language qualification requirements in place. These require them to hire at least one educator holding at least a C1 language qualification in Luxembourgish and at least one educator with the same level in French. Regulations also stipulate that these settings must appoint a pedagogical referent to co-ordinate the implementation of the multilingual education programme. The pedagogical referent must hold a qualification (at least at ISCED Level 3) in the psychosocial, pedagogical or socio-educational fields.

Teachers (*instituteurs*) in formal ECEC must have a bachelor's qualification (ISCED Level 6) in educational sciences or an equivalent qualification. To enter the profession, all teachers must pass a national exam (*concours d'admission*) and complete a three-year stage organised by the National Institute for Continuous Professional Development (IFEN). In the first (non-compulsory) year of formal ECEC (*éducation précoce*), teachers can be supported in their work by other staff (*éducateurs gradués* and *éducateurs diplômés*). Educators (*éducateurs gradués*) are requested to have a bachelor's degree in social and educational sciences (ISCED Level 6). Assistants (*éducateurs diplômés*) must have an ISCED Level 3 qualification.

ECEC staff in Luxembourg often conduct their initial education in foreign countries, particularly in neighbouring countries such as Belgium, France and Germany. Mechanisms are in place to recognise foreign diplomas for staff and teachers in both the non-formal and formal sectors. A commission in MENJE evaluates candidate diplomas and may grant a full or partial recognition, which may require the practitioner to complete additional modules. To work in the formal sector, teachers who conducted their initial education outside Luxembourg must pass a preliminary language test in Luxembourgish, German and French, in addition to the national exam.

The minimum qualification required to become a leader of a centre-based ECEC structure for children under 3 is a bachelor's degree (ISCED Level 6). However, regulations (*Règlement grand-ducal modifié du 14 novembre 2013*) stipulate that an educator with an ISCED Level 3 qualification (*éducateur diplômé*) can also become a leader in settings with fewer than 40 children. Leadership responsibilities in the formal ECEC sector are shared between regional directors, who are required to have a master's degree (ISCED Level 7), and presidents of school committees, who are elected from among the teachers in their schools and therefore have the same qualification as teachers (ISCED Level 6). Regional directors provide oversight and monitoring, whereas school committee presidents focus more on day-to-day functioning and providing overall support for the teachers in their schools.

In past years, Luxembourg has worked to upskill its workforce through continuous professional development. The government provides contracted settings with funding to support staff attendance at trainings. In addition, a reform introduced in 2022 makes continuous training, coaching and mentoring free of charge for all settings, as discussed in detail below.

Requirements for minimum attendance at trainings are in place for all types of settings, with requirements to participate for all categories of ECEC staff working with children of all ages, including the youngest. In non-formal ECEC, 32 hours of professional development over 2 years are required for all staff working with children, and this requirement is linked to the setting's eligibility for the CSA funding programme (see Chapter 1). A specific 30-hour training course to support multilingualism is required for pedagogical referents and is offered free of charge by SNJ. In formal ECEC, compulsory, ongoing training (40 hours per year for assistants, 48 hours over 3 years for teachers) follows the priorities defined by the Ministry of Education, Children and Youth and is offered mainly through IFEN.

Home-based providers in Luxembourg must register with MENJE to benefit from the CSA scheme. From the introduction of the CSA scheme in 2009 until 2016, the number of registered home-based providers increased. From 2017, however, with the introduction of quality requirements, the number of registered providers started decreasing. Home-based providers must conduct 40 hours of continuous professional training every 2 years, of which 20 hours must be training in accordance with the national curriculum framework for non-formal education. Professional development for childminders is provided by the Agence Dageselteren, which is part of Arcus, a non-profit organisation providing services for children, youth and families in the social sector.

Higher qualified and better-prepared staff tend to concentrate in the formal sector and in non-formal contracted settings

The qualification requirements for formal ECEC settings imply that higher qualified staff work in this sector than the non-formal sector. In the non-formal sector, attracting and retaining highly qualified staff is particularly challenging for non-contracted settings, as they offer less advantageous working conditions than contracted settings and the formal sector.

The significant expansion of the ECEC sector in the last ten years has not been followed by a greater availability of qualified ECEC staff trained in Luxembourg. As a result, ECEC providers increasingly rely on staff trained abroad, which may have implications on their preparedness to implement the Luxembourgish curricula and on their knowledge of the Luxembourgish language. With the introduction of higher standards for quality and the curriculum for non-formal education, the gap between required qualifications and the characteristics of available staff has widened.

In particular, some non-contracted settings for the youngest children tend to hire staff who have obtained their diplomas for pre-primary education (*école maternelle*) in France, who often implement pedagogical practices that may be more formal than those suggested in the Luxembourgish non-formal curriculum framework, especially for the youngest children. Non-contracted settings for children under age 4 also struggle to comply with the language qualification requirements for staff (at least one person with C1 level in French and one with the same level in Luxembourgish).

Monitoring settings' compliance with staff minimum qualification requirements is currently not systematic for all types of settings (see Chapter 3). In non-formal education settings serving children aged 0-4, controls are made in compliance with the requirements of the CSA scheme. However, for other settings, while officers from MENJE might ask setting leaders to show proof of staff diplomas if there are particular issues to check, there are no structured controls. It is therefore not clear whether they comply with the minimum requirements for staff languages and qualifications. Implementing a system for consistent monitoring and collection of data in all settings would be important.

Meeting the ECEC objectives of the country requires a broad strategy to further professionalise the workforce

Luxembourg aims to achieve broad enrolment of children in ECEC starting from an early age. It has adopted an ambitious curriculum framework for non-formal education and aspires to promote multilingual education for all with an introduction to Luxembourgish. It considers ECEC a building block to education and central to setting all citizens on a lifelong learning pathway. This ambitious agenda requires strong professionals in the ECEC sector. As the country welcomes children from cross-border workers and includes a large immigrant population who does not necessarily speak Luxembourgish, being able to offer enough places in high-quality ECEC settings is another challenge. This challenge is mainly linked to the difficulty of training and recruiting a sufficiently large number of professionals.

Strengthening the initial education programmes that prepare staff to work in the ECEC sector is an essential element of a strategy to professionalise the workforce. Programmes currently have a broad focus and are not specific to ECEC. Continuous professional development is also fundamental to raising staff skills and knowledge and ensuring that staff who obtained their diplomas abroad have understood and can implement the Luxembourgish vision for non-formal education. In the non-formal sector, the required qualifications for staff are relatively low. Moreover, a heterogeneity of diplomas allows entry into the ECEC profession, which means that staff enter the sector with different backgrounds, attitudes, values and beliefs. This can pose challenges for building a unified vision of ECEC and reaching the high level of quality sought by the national framework for non-formal education.

Currently, continuous professional development does not provide certifications enabling staff to obtain higher qualifications. Defining paths for upskilling staff already working in the ECEC sector would help lead to a more skilled workforce. These elements of a strategy to professionalise the workforce are discussed further in this chapter.

Initial education and preparation

Context

While staff qualifications levels matter, not all research finds a direct link between higher levels of qualification and higher process quality (von Suchodoletz et al., 2017[6]), thus the importance of content and delivery of initial education and professional development trainings (OECD, 2021[1]). In terms of initial education, staff access to specialised education in ECEC has been linked with improved process quality (OECD, 2018[2]).

In Luxembourg, there are no ECEC-specific initial education programmes. The vocational secondary institution (*Lycée technique pour professions éducatives et sociales,* LTPES) offers a general training programme that prepares professionals to work in the social field, including with children, the elderly, and people with disabilities and special needs. This programme lasts three years (the two last years of secondary education plus one extra year) and offers a qualification at the ISCED Level 3 (*éducateur diplômé*).

At the higher education level, the University of Luxembourg offers a bachelor's degree in social and educational sciences, from which students graduate as social assistant professionals. This diploma (ISCED Level 6, *éducateur gradué*) is a broad qualification for social pedagogical work with all age groups. It allows an individual to work as an educator in both the formal and non-formal sectors. The University of Luxembourg also offers a bachelor's degree in educational sciences (ISCED Level 6) that is required to become a teacher in the formal sector.

The Ministry for Higher Education and Research holds main policy responsibility for the quality of initial training in both further and higher education. Although the Ministry for Higher Education and Research has regular exchanges with the University of Luxembourg and the LTPES, there are no explicitly defined quality standards for initial education programmes, and the University of Luxembourg has large autonomy. Initial education institutions have procedures for internal evaluation, but there are no mechanisms in place for the external monitoring of the programmes.

Initial education programmes could offer a stronger focus on ECEC

Since initial education programmes have broad objectives, graduates from these programmes are often not familiar with the national curriculum frameworks for ECEC. They may also not have been trained on pedagogical approaches with young children. While the content of the ISCED 6 programmes seems more aligned with national curriculum frameworks for ECEC, the ISCED 3 degree does not systematically include this content. Staff with higher qualifications, who have a better understanding of curriculum framework, often have more responsibility roles and are less in contact with children, which may have implications for quality.

Providers of initial education for ECEC staff have the autonomy to organise their programmes and define their curriculum frameworks. MENJE should, however, go beyond informal collaboration and define long-term quality standards for initial education programmes, including a stronger alignment with national curricula for ECEC. These standards should be defined collaboratively in consultation with experts and the ECEC sector. At a later stage, monitoring should be implemented to ensure that initial education programmes are compliant with the defined standards.

Particularly in the non-formal sector, it is essential to ensure that the LTPES programme further incorporates the vision of non-formal education. Ensuring that all students in initial education who aim to work in the ECEC field receive training on the curriculum framework for non-formal education is vital to preparing them to work with young children.

However, since the LTPES programme has a broad scope, there are limits to the extent to which ECEC topics can be integrated. It might be worth exploring the possibility of reviewing the programme in order to grant specialisations in the qualification that would allow students to take a more specialised path. One mechanism would be to create an ECEC track within the programme and enable students interested in working in ECEC to choose courses aligned with the skills and knowledge needed to work in ECEC. A specialised track can also be implemented by making it possible to specialise in ECEC in the last year of the programme, with relevant courses or work-based trainings/apprenticeships. A final option, which could replace or complement the two first mechanisms, would be to add a year for (further) specialisation.

In the current LTPES programme, further efforts could be made to intentionally align the already existing modules covering ECEC with the principles of the curriculum framework for non-formal education. Another way to more broadly incorporate the vision for non-formal education into the LTPES programme is to highlight the rationale that although the curriculum framework for non-formal education encompasses children and youth up to age 18, its general principles (e.g. autonomy, well-being, participation) can also apply to other populations in the social field.

Practicums are included in initial education programmes, but a focus on the ECEC sector could be expanded

Research has long highlighted the critical role played by work-based training for sustaining situated and context-based learning (Balduzzi and Lazzari, 2015[7]; Flämig, König and Spiekermann, 2015[8]). As prospective staff engage in hands-on activities and deal with the challenges of everyday practice, they are provided with opportunities to build and apply new knowledge in real-life situations (Kaarby and Lindboe, 2016[9]). The OECD Teaching and Learning International Survey (TALIS) *Starting Strong 2018* (an international survey of ECEC staff) suggests that initial preparation that includes a practical component tends to expose staff to a broader range of content, in particular in areas that are otherwise less commonly integrated into programmes, such as working with a diversity of children or classroom management (OECD, 2020[10]). Data from the *Quality beyond Regulations* project (OECD, 2021[1]) show that in participating countries, a practicum is required in most settings covering children aged 3-5, as well as in most of those for ages 0-5. However, they are less frequent in settings for children aged 0-2 (Figure 2.2).

Initial education programmes in Luxembourg include a practicum component. At the University of Luxembourg, the bachelor's degree in social and educational sciences includes two internships: one conducted in the second semester and another in the sixth semester.

ECEC staff who start working in the formal sector also go through a two-year induction period at the beginning of their assignment. In the non-formal sector, induction programmes for newly arrived staff seem to depend on each setting and their capacity to train staff. A more systematic approach to induction and coaching would be important (see the "Continuous professional development" section).

In the LTPES programme, students must conduct one internship per year. In the first year, the internship lasts 9 weeks; in the second, 6 weeks; and in the third, 11 weeks. The LTPES has concluded agreements with different types of ECEC settings where students can conduct their internships, both contracted and non-contracted. During the internship, students are supported by a teacher from LTPES and a tutor in the field. The tutor is part of the setting's staff and is required to hold an ISCED 3 qualification and have at least two years of experience to be assigned this role. The LTPES offers support to tutors, such as information meetings, trainings and resources. Tutors also receive an extra salary for conducting this function.

Figure 2.2. Practicum requirements as part of ECEC professionals' initial education and training in OECD countries, 2019

Percentage of settings that require a practicum, by age group and staff type, in all participating countries

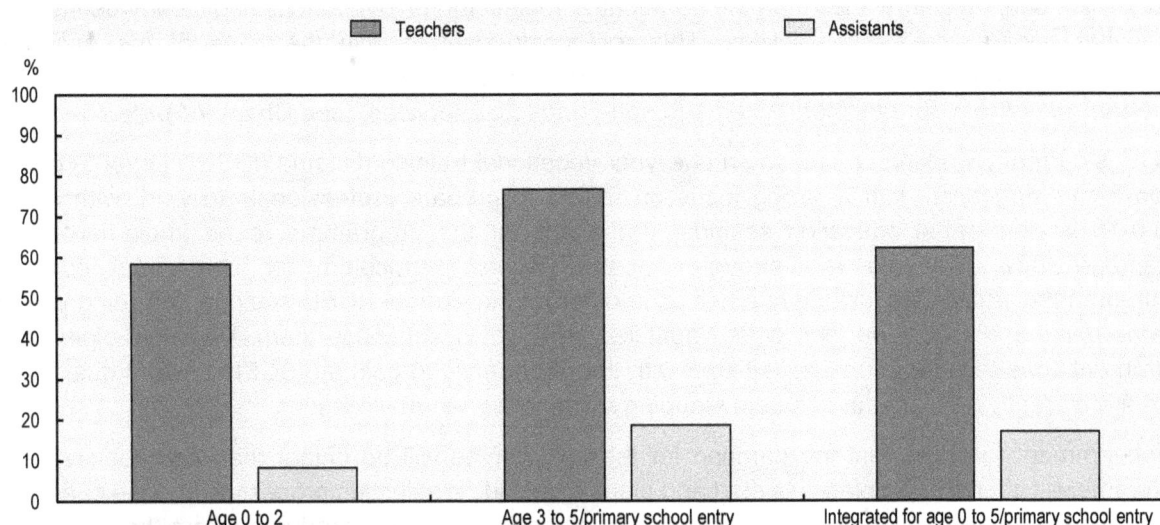

Note: The percentage in each age group is based on the total number of observations/settings within the age group, including settings classified as "not applicable" or "missing".
Source: (OECD, 2021[1])

Given the broad scope of the LTPES programme, the practical placement can take place in any sector of the social field. As internships are often carried out in contexts other than early childhood education settings (and often outside the non-formal sector), graduates often start working without any practical experience in the sector. Ensuring that all students who aim to work in the ECEC field receive practical experience during their initial education is critical to preparing them for working with young children. This could be done by allowing students interested in working in ECEC to conduct several internships in the field of ECEC, for example, within the specialised track discussed earlier.

Expanding options for ECEC initial training to align with different roles can help match the sector's demand, but attention to quality is needed

The ECEC sector in Luxembourg has developed quickly over the last few decades, increasing the demand for a qualified workforce to enter the profession. However, Luxembourg's existing initial education programmes currently produce fewer graduates than the sector needs. For example, from the University of Luxembourg, as the degree does not specialise in ECEC, only around 20% of graduates work in formal ECEC (70 *éducateurs gradués* per year). This represents a small percentage of the demand for ECEC staff.

The pressing need for qualified staff calls for strategies to increase the number of graduates qualified to work in the sector. Beyond the existing offer of initial education programmes, it would be worth exploring the possibility of creating new specific ECEC programmes that provide qualification at ISCED Levels 3 to 6, as there seems to be sufficient demand from prospective students. The availability of specialised programmes (or at least partly specialised) could allow unqualified staff to obtain a qualification and staff with low qualifications to upskill. For example, a new specialised programme (e.g. two-year duration) could allow staff to move from an ISCED 3 to an ISCED 4 and ISCED 5 qualification. This specialised programme could, for example, be integrated into the LTPES programme as an optional extra two years.

Specific ECEC programmes at different levels of education would need to match different roles and responsibilities and could facilitate career progression. For instance, there is room to define the role of staff more clearly with higher educational qualifications and more specific knowledge of the curriculum framework for non-formal education. Staff members now tend to be employed in the non-formal contracted sector, which offers higher wages than the non-contracted sector, but without having clearly defined roles with higher pedagogical responsibilities. This role could overlap with the roles of the multilingual pedagogical referent or with the leader of the setting and would need to be included uniformly in the non-formal sector (e.g. for both contracted and non-contracted services) (see Chapter 1).

MENJE is currently working on creating a one-year vocational training diploma (ISCED Level 3) targeted to non-formal education with a strong focus on ECEC to prepare professionals to work with children aged 0-18 in non-formal education settings. Plans are for the programme to be implemented from September 2022. It would rely strongly on the national curriculum for non-formal education. The programme would also include internships in different non-formal ECEC settings, including *crèches*, *maisons relais* and *foyers de jour*, where qualified staff would supervise them. With this diploma, the government aims to provide unqualified staff with the opportunity to gain an ISCED Level 3 qualification. There are currently no plans for it to be a stepping stone to higher qualifications.

The government foresees that the demand for the programme will be higher than its capacity, as the programme will offer only 60 places to start and plans to include a selection process to choose candidates. The vocational training would be targeted mainly at students who have graduated from the third year of secondary school. This being said, the government is currently collaborating with the *École Nationale pour Adultes* (ENAD) to implement the programme in a way that facilitates the attendance of working adults. However, no specific provisions have been made to target this programme to home-based providers. Communicating the availability of this programme to these providers and offering incentives for their attendance would help foster quality in home-based settings.

While there seems to be a significant potential demand for places in a specialised ECEC initial education programme (as the ECEC profession attracts prospective students), higher education institutions might not have the capacity to provide it. It has been difficult to find the teaching body to provide the trainings on the providers' side. Another challenge has been the limits in their infrastructural capacity to receive more students.

Efforts to find and attract qualified educators to provide initial education programmes are needed, for example, through co-operation with foreign universities. Hybrid models, with both in-person and online modules, can also help increase the capacity of initial education institutions. Another strategy for the non-formal sector could be to allow a higher number of these apprentices beyond the 10% limit for "unqualified staff" in settings serving children under age 4, and beyond 20% in settings serving children above age 4. The review team noted that receiving settings consider students conducting apprenticeships as an important support.

Increasing the capacity of initial education programmes should not be to the detriment of quality. Programmes need to include a good balance between courses and practice. Students need to be mentored and supported, especially during practical experiences and be allowed time for reflection. The content of the vocational programme should also match the sector's priorities. For this, collaboration with SNJ and regional officers will be essential, as they can provide valuable feedback on staff training needs.

Continuous professional development

Context

Continuous professional development is pivotal for ECEC staff to extend and update their knowledge and develop new skills (OECD, 2021[1]; Hamre, Partee and Mulcahy, 2017[11]). Recent studies suggest that staff participation in well-designed professional development can be effective in supporting process quality in ECEC settings, for instance, by enhancing staff's abilities to create close, warm and responsive relationships with children, to manage behaviour and to stimulate children's reasoning and language development (Eckhardt and Egert, 2020[12]; Egert, Dederer and Fukkink, 2020[13]; Markussen-Brown et al., 2017[14]; Werner et al., 2016[15]). Participation in professional development can moreover support the development of staff's professional identity and their well-being, buffer the negative effect of stress and burnout, and boost satisfaction, commitment and retention (Peleman et al., 2018[16]; Sandilos et al., 2018[17]; Totenhagen et al., 2015[18]). Effective adult-learning activities typically exhibit features such as responsiveness to context, a strong evaluative dimension of practice, and individual feedback and guidance (OECD, 2021[1]; Boeskens, Nusche and Yurita, 2020[19]).

Continuous professional development is particularly important in the context of Luxembourg, where staff come from diverse backgrounds and have different qualification levels. Professional development can help upskill the workforce particularly in the non-formal sector and in non-contracted settings, where initial education levels are relatively low.

Besides training ECEC staff on specific themes, pedagogies and practices, continuous professional development helps foster values, attitudes and beliefs on ECEC and is necessary for ECEC staff to develop a shared understanding of ECEC in alignment with national curriculum frameworks. Most graduates entering the ECEC sector in Luxembourg do not have specialised education in ECEC and are also not familiar with non-formal education. In addition, such trainings are crucial for staff who have conducted their initial education in foreign countries and may have different visions.

Continuous professional development is also vital for ECEC staff who graduated some time ago and did not receive any initial education on curriculum frameworks. Training can ensure that working staff keep updated on the latest developments in the field, which is necessary considering the significant changes introduced in the sector in the last ten years.

All ECEC staff in Luxembourg are required to participate in continuous professional development for a minimum amount of time, in both the formal sector (40 hours per year for educators; 48 hours over 3 years for teachers) and the non-formal sector (32 hours over 2 years for all staff). Training requirements are the same for newly arrived staff and experienced ones. In addition, in the non-formal sector, a specific training on multilingualism (30 hours) is compulsory for pedagogical officers, and specific trainings on inclusion are also offered. Bigger providers tend to have a comprehensive offer of training for their leaders and networks that support them in their role, but this is not the case for most settings.

In formal ECEC, continuous professional development is overseen by MENJE. Compulsory ongoing training is offered mainly through IFEN, which is also responsible for induction and coaching and which works closely with the Service for Co-ordination of Research and Pedagogical and Technological Innovation (SCRIPT) department. IFEN provides courses for teachers and educators (both together and separately).

Until recently, the government has only paid for continuous professional development training in the non-formal sector for contracted settings, while non-contracted settings were not receiving funding beyond the one provided through the subsidy funding scheme (CSA). However, since the beginning of 2022, the cost of trainings is now funded by the government for all providers in the non-formal sector. Continuous professional development in the non-formal sector is delivered by several agencies, including Arcus, Caritas, Croix rouge, Elisabeth, and Inter-Actions, which are all part of the FEDAS (which is both a federation and an agency). ECEC leaders can also arrange with providers to deliver the trainings in their particular setting. The agencies also offer coaching for leaders and supervision of teams.

At the time of writing, the government was advancing on a reform to re-organise and harmonise the continuous professional development system in the non-formal sector. The reform process is overseen by a commission with several stakeholders, including representatives of the ECEC settings, employees, MENJE and SNJ. The new system coming into force in 2022 is co-ordinated by SNJ and covers all types of settings and staff (including home-based).

One objective of the reform is to increase participation in training. Since 1 January 2022, continuous professional development in the non-formal sector is financed by the government for contracted and non-contracted settings and for all types of staff (including qualified and unqualified). To benefit from the free-of-charge programme, each ECEC setting is asked to outline an annual programme for its staff. Settings are also requested to provide a list of their staff in order to receive credits according to the number of staff. Credits are equivalent to 24 hours a year per full-time staff, which is above the minimum requirement for professional development (32 hours in two years). Staff time to attend trainings still have to be covered by providers.

There are also plans to reform professional development for home-based providers. The aim is to improve the quality of trainings, responding to home-based providers' particular needs. Different formats of training are considered and could be provided, including courses, practical exercises and coaching.

As part of the government reform, monitoring for compliance with the minimum hours of training is placed under the responsibility of MENJE and is no longer part of regional officers' functions (see Chapter 3). However, regional officers will have to evaluate the training and professional development annual plans of each ECEC setting to ensure that they are adapted to their profile and needs.

Staff and leaders participation in continuous professional development needs to increase in the non-formal ECEC sector

In the non-formal education sector, there is a comprehensive offer of professional development trainings for staff. However, one barrier for staff to attend trainings is that providers have to cover for staff time, and they often struggle to find replacements for staff in training. The fact that all staff working with children require the same number of hours means that centres do not have much flexibility in assigning training to staff who need it more. For non-contracted settings, the costs of continuous professional development trainings might have been a significant barrier, which created an imbalance within the non-formal ECEC sector.

The payment of training courses by the government for all types of settings starting in 2022 can help reduce inequality in treatment of the formal and non-formal sectors and should support continuous professional development in non-contracted settings and small settings. The inclusion of home-based providers in the plan is also an essential step in professionalising the sector and raising their skills. By supporting broader participation in training, the credits system would also help progressively overcome heterogeneity in staff's backgrounds and qualifications.

From the staff's point of view, other potential barriers to participation in professional development may include: not having the time, either for work or family reasons; the fact that there is no compensation for staff absences during training; or they might not see the benefits of training. If participation in training remains below the requirement after implementing the reform, data could be collected to understand the reasons for non-participation.

Given that leaders' initial training does not include specialised content on ECEC, nor on managerial skills, ensuring the quality of continuous professional development training for leaders can help them be better qualified for their tasks. Leaders of ECEC settings have an essential role to play in providing the conditions for staff to develop high-quality practices, for instance, by building a climate of trust and collaboration, facilitating staff engagement in professional learning and addressing sources of stress for staff in their work (OECD, 2021[1]; Douglass, 2019[20]). Findings from the TALIS *Starting Strong 2018* survey show that in centres where leaders set a clear vision, staff report a stronger sense of self-efficacy (OECD, 2020[21]). Leadership is also crucial for translating policies into practice and driving innovation and change in systems (OECD, 2019[22]; 2015[23]).

The reform of the system includes strategies to support the professional development of leaders. This includes coaching, mentoring and a diverse offer of training courses. Some topics that would be relevant for training content include management practices; implementing curriculum frameworks; supporting staff with their pedagogical work; fostering self-reflection in their settings; and engaging with parents, communities and the formal education sector.

Continuous professional development should further adapt to staff and leaders' training needs

The offer of trainings includes a variety of course topics. However, there seems to be a mismatch between the content of continuous professional development trainings and staff training needs. For example, staff seem to request further training and support in implementing curriculum frameworks, and the provision of this type of training seems not to meet the demand. A survey on training needs conducted by SNJ shows that staff also express the need for more courses on topics such as inclusion and multilingual education and more face-to-face rather than virtual trainings. Trainings on multilingualism are provided to pedagogical referents within settings, but not necessarily to other staff, and they are not enough to cater for the important demand. Another issue is that pedagogical referents struggle to transmit their training to the rest of the staff in their settings.

Increasing the offer of training courses for unqualified staff (maximum 10% per setting serving children under age 4 and 20% per setting serving children above 4) and targeting high-quality training specific to them should be considered within the review plans. The new credits system gives ECEC centre leaders the possibility to allocate more training to the staff who need it.

The offer of trainings for leaders is limited. In particular, leaders are not receiving enough training on the curriculum framework for non-formal education. They also need further training on management practices. The survey on training needs conducted by SNJ shows that leaders need further coaching and individual support. For example, a new pilot programme implemented by the FEDAS, with support of SNJ, to support leaders has been well attended.

Language of provision of trainings also seems to be an issue, as there are often not enough trainings in French available, which is a problem, particularly for non-contracted settings that are more likely to employ French-speaking staff. Some staff may also welcome more trainings in English.

As the government is advancing with reforms to increase funding for continuous professional development, it is vital to ensure that training content is aligned with staff needs. Training that focuses on ECEC content and the national frameworks and has a practical orientation (e.g. how to talk with children, interactions within guided play) can help staff better understand the principles of non-formal and multilingual education.

The 2022 reform intends to develop a coherent and diverse set of courses and adjust the training content to staff and leaders' training needs. The agencies providing the trainings will be asked to submit a programme for their training offer, which will be evaluated for approval by SNJ against quality standards. The offer will also include trainings that are not directly linked to the national curriculum framework. A commission chaired by SNJ and including other stakeholders, the "Further Training Commission", is charged with overseeing the system's reform, co-ordinating the provision of training from the agencies, and ensuring that continuous professional development responds to the needs of the sector.

With this new approach, care needs to be taken to ensure that mechanisms are in place to assess the training needs of staff and leaders and that training provision responds to these needs. SNJ plans to collect information on staff training needs through surveys. Collecting data on training needs as well as staff backgrounds, qualifications and language proficiency will help inform the design of training programmes. SNJ also plans to consult regional officers and involve them in the review process of the continuous professional development system. According to the results of their monitoring visits, their expertise can help inform the training course programmes on the areas where staff need further support. Feedback from SNJ staff directly involved in the provision of training, such as for multilingual education, will also be valuable in designing the content of the continuous professional development offer.

In the non-formal sector, the decision on who does the training and what they do is taken by leaders. While some leaders provide staff flexibility, others choose trainings for their staff according to their own considerations. The OECD review team noted disagreement between staff and leaders in some cases. There could be more clarity on training objectives, especially on the balance to be found between addressing the needs of staff members for their own development or addressing the more short-term needs of the centre. Regional officers also have a role to play in advising on training needs, taking into account the various interests (see Chapter 3).

Attention to the format and quality of continuous professional development is needed

In developing the reform of the system, attention should be given to alternative formats of professional development. In addition to traditional training courses, mentoring and coaching have been shown to effectively lead to improvement in practices with young children and can therefore be well adapted to the Luxembourgish context where staff are expected to implement high-quality practices according to the curriculum framework. The credits system, which allocates funding to cover more hours of training than the legal requirement, will provide ECEC centre leaders with the flexibility to use the extra credits for various formats of training, such as coaching or group training. The new system can finance hours of pedagogical support (mentoring and coaching from trainers) and professional support (team supervision and facilitation in case of conflicts).

Induction programmes can also familiarise staff with different backgrounds and qualifications with the setting and the sector. Induction periods could include a theoretical part on the goals, values and vision of non-formal ECEC. This would require ECEC centre leaders to be trained to be able to support newly arrived staff throughout this period.

More attention needs to be put on monitoring the quality of professional development. As agencies will be required to fulfil quality standards set by the Further Training Commission, systematic mechanisms need to be set to monitor the quality of the training provision.

The reform of professional development includes efforts to strengthen the quality of training provision through criteria for training structure, content and methods. The new training system will be evaluated by the end of 2022 and revised as needed (2022 will be considered a transition year). ECEC providers will be required to present a training plan for their setting, which from 2023 will need to be validated by regional officers, in line with feedback previously provided and with the setting's internal evaluation. The aim is for setting leaders to take stronger responsibility for their staff's development.

SNJ is also developing standards for trainers in terms of qualifications and background. Trainers will have to be accredited by each agency, based on criteria set by the Further Training Commission, which SNJ chairs. As in initial education, finding competent trainers to provide continuous professional development trainings in the non-formal sector has proven difficult. Strategies need to be put in place to recruit qualified trainers who have good knowledge of the national curriculum framework for non-formal education, as well as trainers who can deliver courses in French. For this, co-operation with the initial education sector might provide opportunities for cross-fertilisation.

There is also little communication between initial training providers and continuous professional development providers. Fostering co-operation between the two can be useful to ensure complementarity and to identify gaps and areas where staff may need further support. MENJE could further engage with the University of Luxembourg and LTPES, which would better inform the design of continuous professional development training programmes.

Continuing co-operation with Agence Dageselteren is key to ensuring that home-based provider training is consistent with training for staff in centre-based settings. In particular, home-based providers seem to request further support with conducting administrative processes. These providers also need support in applying quality pedagogical practices with children and becoming familiar with the national framework for non-formal education.

Continuous professional development could help to raise formal qualifications of ECEC staff

Strengthening co-operation between professional development providers and initial training providers can help to develop professional development certification. Continuous professional development does not provide certification and is not linked with possible career pathways in Luxembourg. Developing certification of professional development and possibly a system of micro-credits that could be obtained through participation in several modules would help less qualified staff to gain qualifications and ultimately improve their interactions with children. Such a system would also encourage training providers to design short programmes (or modules) that can be combined with others in a consistent programme. This could increase the quality of professional development while providing incentives to staff to participate in obtaining a higher qualification and possibly earning higher wages.

Such a system would also allow staff to upgrade their qualifications while still working and combine courses and work-based learning. It could also be adapted to qualified working staff (*éducateurs diplômés*) to upskill to an ISCED 4 or 5 level through this process.

The lack of a specialised programme in ECEC is a challenge for working staff who wish to upgrade their qualifications to ISCED Levels 4 and 5. Furthermore, mechanisms for recognition of prior learning are not widespread and appear complex, which may be preventing staff with experience and relevant skillsets to upgrade their qualifications.

The plans to reform continuous professional development offer a good opportunity to design paths for upskilling working staff. For instance, designing a programme that allows staff to upgrade their qualifications, building on training modules in addition to work-based learning. For working staff with an ISCED 3 qualification (*éducateur diplômé*), this plan could aim to translate prior experience and continuous training into an ISCED 4 and 5 qualifications and to upskill to an ISCED 6 qualification (*éducateur gradué*). For unqualified staff who are working, the reform of the system could consider strategies to enable them to obtain an ISCED 3 qualification through training completion.

Staff preparedness to apply curriculum frameworks

Context

The curriculum framework for non-formal education (*Cadre de référence national sur l'éducation non formelle des enfants et des jeunes*) provides guidance for staff and leaders working with children aged 0-12 in non-formal institutions. The curriculum for the formal sector (*Plan d'études de l'école fondamentale*) covers both pre-primary and primary schooling, with a separate supplement for the first, non-compulsory year of formal education (*Plan cadre pour l'éducation précoce*). The curricula for formal and non-formal education are seen as complementary. Both frameworks share a child-centred approach, with a strong emphasis on play and a commitment to enhancing diversity, inclusion, and multilingualism. Process quality is given a central place in both curricula. They are also very much aligned in terms of areas of action.

With three national languages, multilingualism is an important component of life in Luxembourg, including for ECEC. Multilingual education is an important component of both formal and non-formal education curricula. The multilingual programme for non-formal education aims to familiarise children with the Luxembourgish language from an early age and to foster the use of children's home languages in ECEC settings. The programme also places importance on co-operation with parents and linkages with communities. The multilingual programme for non-formal education is based on research and is supported by a scientific council formed by experts from different countries. ECEC centres in the non-formal sector are required to apply the multilingual programme as part of the CSA scheme, which requires them to have at least one staff with a level C1 in Luxembourgish and one with a level C1 in French.

As part of the multilingual programme, settings must comply with a specific training on multilingualism for their pedagogical referents (30 hours) and all staff (8 hours every 2 years). These training courses are organised by SNJ. The multilingual programme provides high-quality trainings (for example, including concrete examples of pedagogical practices while also stressing the need to cater to the needs of the child).

The government provides different types of resources to help staff to understand the national curriculum framework for non-formal education. This includes publishing guides to accompany the curriculum framework and making the framework messages more accessible to staff. A comprehensive set of publications, available in different languages and targeted at different audiences, aims to make the curriculum accessible to the different profiles of staff and parents. All publications are freely accessible through the SNJ platform (http://www.enfancejeunesse.lu/). SNJ also aims to translate complex content into plain language by preparing videos and posters for staff and booklets for parents.

The curriculum framework for non-formal education is a milestone for the sector, but further efforts are needed to prepare staff to implement it

The curriculum framework for non-formal education is very well regarded by all stakeholders in Luxembourg, as it has an educational component and also focuses on well-being. The framework is considered a strength of the system and a building block for quality. ECEC staff in the non-formal sector also consider that the curriculum framework gives legitimacy and value to the educational work they are conducting.

However, staff still seem to struggle to fully understand and implement the ambitious goals and sophisticated approach of the curriculum framework for non-formal education. Reports from regional officers show that this is the case, particularly in non-contracted settings. Several factors can explain staff challenges to fully implement all aspects of the curriculum. Changing deeply rooted beliefs, values and attitudes on ECEC held by staff is a difficult task that demands time and resources. Stakeholders in the sector feel that when the curriculum was first introduced, it was done rapidly and in a top-down approach. Although many initiatives were implemented subsequently by the government to train and support staff in this new framework, getting all ECEC staff on board with the new vision for the sector will require further effort.

There is a significant gap between staff preparedness and the high expectations for quality in the curriculum framework, particularly in the non-contracted sector. Most staff have not received any preparation on the framework during their initial education; therefore, it is not clear whether they sufficiently understand the concept of non-formal education. Despite the available offer of continuous professional development training and material resources, it seems that some staff are still not familiar with the curriculum framework. The curriculum framework for non-formal education seems particularly hard to understand for home-based settings staff, for example.

The OECD review team noted that in some cases, staff approaches to ECEC remain focused on planned activities and children's outcomes, in a formal fashion. Important concepts of the curriculum framework might not be clear to staff, including child participation, child competency, multilingualism and play. However, since there is no systematic monitoring of this (see Chapter 3), the extent to which practices align with the curriculum framework is not completely clear. Staff could also be better prepared to use the logbook as a basis for self-reflection, not only to enter activities. There are also difficulties in the design of settings' pedagogical concepts. Staff working with children are not always involved in this task, making it hard for them to fully understand the concept and feel ownership.

Furthermore, the first version of the curriculum was drafted in a rather complex, academic language, which many stakeholders found hard to understand. Despite efforts made by SNJ to publish targeted publications that simplify the curriculum's content and include practical examples, ECEC staff still struggle to translate the curriculum expectations into their daily practices with children, and adapt them to the child and families needs. It is unclear how much the different publications are used by staff and providers of continuous professional development training. There could also be more guidance for providers of professional development training to use these publications.

Another difficulty is that some providers, in particular, big structures, seem to have their own pedagogical approaches that are not always or fully aligned with the national curriculum framework. In settings where providers insist in taking a different pedagogical approach, it can be difficult to align staff practices with the curriculum through quality support and training. Strengthening the monitoring and quality assurance system to address this issue is important to ensure the implementation of the curriculum framework (see Chapter 3).

Staff also need further support in engaging with parents and in supporting transitions within ECEC. Many parents are not familiar with the national curriculum for non-formal education. They might have expectations that are not aligned with the goals of the curriculum framework, for example, that non-formal settings provide only care, overlooking the educational component. Alternatively, they might have expectations for children's outcomes that correspond to formal education.

Staff need more tools to explain to parents the non-formal education vision, the pedagogies used in the setting and the important educational work they conduct. To prepare them to do this, training courses are needed on how to communicate with parents on children's development and how to integrate them better in the life of the ECEC setting. In addition, staff need further preparation on how they can engage with parents to help them work with children from various backgrounds.

To support children's transitions across different types of settings and across formal and non-formal settings, it is important to support staff in both sectors to understand the importance of the continuity of children's experiences. Trainings can prepare staff across levels on the different developmental needs of children at different stages. Information on the singularities of different settings (particularly of non-formal vs formal) can also help staff support continuity. For example, it would be important to ensure that children aged 3-4 who stay in the non-formal sector (instead of going to *précoce*) receive stimulating, age-appropriate practices that support them to move on to the formal sector. More systematic information for staff on the different settings children attend (sometimes in the same day) would also be helpful to staff.

Recent initiatives to review the curriculum framework can help make it more accessible and practical for staff

A revised version of the framework was finalised and launched at the end of 2021. This revised version of the framework aims at more consistency and simplification of the text. It also includes new chapters on topics that were under-developed previously (e.g. on children's rights). The framework review was informed by feedback from the sector and overviewed by a commission set up by SNJ and MENJE. A new flyer synthesising the framework has been prepared for staff, and a paper for parents is also in preparation. Although this revised version was launched recently, a further review of the curriculum framework for non-formal education is planned for 2022.

The next version of the framework is scheduled for 2024/25. This version will further simplify the text and include more practical examples. Consultations with the local ECEC structures via working groups are planned to incorporate their views into the new framework. The process, which aims to move away from a sometimes-abstract language to a register that can resonate with ECEC staff, is an important step forward to improving curriculum implementation. ECEC staff might also find the inclusion of practical examples to explain complex concepts helpful. For example, illustrating child participation with concrete examples of interactions with children might facilitate understanding this notion.

The government has started discussions with providers of initial education and professional development to further include the curriculum framework for non-formal education in their programmes, but further efforts are needed, particularly for initial education (see the "Initial education and preparation" section).

New training on the curriculum framework for non-formal education targets staff working in the formal education sector. SNJ is currently piloting this in co-operation with IFEN. The training aim to help school staff understand the approach of non-formal education and its differences with formal education. The objective is to foster the continuity of children's experiences and improve collaboration across sectors.

The review of the continuous professional development system can help staff to implement the multilingual programme

The multilingual programme for non-formal education is ambitious and sophisticated, based on research and best practices for children of ECEC age. Luxembourg also has a highly innovative approach to multilingualism and devotes impressive means (and policies) to this objective. In recent years, staff attitudes towards multilingualism and children's home languages have improved significantly. Before implementing the programme, not only were home languages not encouraged to be used by children and ECEC staff, but studies have shown that they may have been forbidden. Nowadays, most ECEC staff have a good understanding of multilingual education principles and welcome children's home languages.

Some challenges remain for the proper implementation of the multilingual programme. Some staff still feel unprepared to proficiently speak the main languages used in Luxembourg, which interferes with their ability to create an enabling environment for children to use these languages. Staff need further support in understanding that the objective of multilingual education is to interact with children and have an attitude that encourages the use of languages beyond staff's own proficiency. Staff need preparation to offer children opportunities to interact in their home languages beyond formal activities, and to avoid stereotypical characterisation of languages and cultures. Staff could be further trained on establishing more frequent and meaningful conversations with children and better communicating the programme's goals to families.

Furthermore, although all home languages are accepted in ECEC settings in general, studies from the University of Luxembourg note that an implicit hierarchy of languages exists. Staff in some settings will insist on speaking mostly Luxembourgish (or French, depending on the settings type). English, German, Portuguese, Italian and Spanish seem to be common languages used in some settings. However, some of the children's home languages often remain hidden, e.g. Arabic, Mandarin or Persian. Given that staff do not usually speak these languages, they might feel uncomfortable fostering their use. Further efforts in monitoring are needed to understand the nature of interactions and languages spoken in ECEC settings (see Chapter 3).

In non-contracted settings, the programme for multilingualism can be more challenging to implement. As many of the private *crèches* are managed by French-speaking leaders and contract mainly

French-speaking staff, they face challenges in applying the notions of multilingualism. These settings tend to plan specific hours to do languages (e.g. the Luxembourgish hour or German hour), or they assign specific staff to a particular language (e.g. one person who speaks only Luxembourgish to the children) as they lack the qualified staff to fully implement the programme for multilingualism.

Additional training is needed to support staff in implementing the programme for multilingualism across settings. While the trainings provided by SNJ to pedagogical referents seem to be of high quality, the offer seems insufficient for the demand. It also seems that pedagogical referents find it difficult to transmit the vision and knowledge on multilingualism to the rest of the staff in their settings.

With the review of the continuous professional development system, SNJ should be able to increase its offer of courses. There are plans to hire experts to provide these trainings. They also plan to implement blended learning to reach more staff. The training would have a virtual part on theory and an in-person module where staff could bring videos with examples of their own practice. This type of training can help work with staff on their attitudes and beliefs on multilingualism.

Further communication between the SNJ's Innovation Division, including the multilingual team, and the regional officers is needed to inform the programme's implementation. Regional officers can provide valuable feedback on how the programme is being implemented in the field. While currently, this communication seems to be taking place only informally, a more structured approach is planned for 2022. Co-operation with the formal sector is also needed to ensure continuity (children transition across the two multiple times, even in the same day). This can be fostered, for example, by encouraging representatives of the formal sector to attend meetings of the scientific advisory board that oversees the multilingual programme. Providing incentives to staff from both sectors to attend training on multilingualism together (for example, at IFEN) could be very helpful in ensuring coherence in the approach across the sector.

Working conditions

Context

Staff working conditions have an impact on staff well-being, in particular on their emotional well-being, which in turn has an effect on their practices with children and their performance at work. Overall, staff working conditions and well-being can be important drivers of process quality. They can also determine job quality (Cazes, Hijzen and Saint-Martin, 2015[24]), which might, in turn, be a reason for candidates to join the sector, and for existing staff to stay or leave, finally determining the capacity of the sector to retain high-quality staff. Working conditions include various aspects, such as earnings, job security and career prospects, workload and the quality of the working environment at the ECEC centre.

Research shows that salaries are a crucial component of working conditions and for attracting and retaining ECEC staff. Several studies also find a relationship between salaries and the quality of staff's interactions with children, with better-paid staff having more sensitive interactions with children and fewer detached ones (Cassidy et al., 2017[25]; Hu et al., 2017[26]). This is also the case in home-based settings (Eckhardt and Egert, 2020[12]). Teachers' perceptions regarding the fairness of their wages are also positively correlated with process quality (Cassidy et al., 2017[25]). Results from TALIS *Starting Strong 2018* on nine participating countries show that staff have low satisfaction with salaries and that this associates with stress and disengagement with work (OECD, 2020[10]).

The quality of a working environment also includes non-economic aspects of jobs, such as the nature and content of the tasks at hand and working-time arrangements (Cazes, Hijzen and Saint-Martin, 2015[24]). A heavy workload with multiple, ongoing tasks that demand persistent physical, psychological or emotional efforts can lead to less engagement and commitment, with detrimental effects on classroom or playgroup practices (Ansari et al., 2020[27]). There is empirical evidence suggesting that excessive demands and work overload (i.e. high demand, not enough time, shortage of assistance) are negatively associated with process quality (Aboagye et al., 2020[28]; Aboagye et al., 2020[29]; Chen, Phillips and Izci, 2018[30]). ECEC staff work includes a variety of responsibilities and activities that go beyond working directly with children, including individual planning or preparing play and learning activities; collaborating and speaking with colleagues and parents or guardians; documenting children's development, well-being and learning; attending professional development activities; and administrative tasks. Some countries have regulations to ensure that staff have paid time allocated to tasks to be performed without children, generally more often for teachers than assistants (OECD, 2021[1]).

In Luxembourg, working conditions for ECEC staff are more advantageous in the formal sector than in the non-formal sector. In the formal sector, teachers' contracts are full-time, and they receive the same wages as their colleagues from primary school, which are the highest salaries in all OECD countries. Pre-primary teachers have a relatively low number of teaching days (176 days per year) compared to other OECD countries (194 days per year, on average) (OECD, 2020[31]). Teachers in the formal sector have all the benefits of civil servant status, including longer vacations. Within the formal sector, though, conditions are different for teachers (*instituteurs*) and other categories of ECEC staff working in *précoce*. Educators who hold an ISCED 3 and 6 qualification (*educateurs gradués et diplomés*) have a different status and type of contract to teachers, as well as a lower salary. They often have part-time contracts.

In the non-formal sector, staff often have part-time contracts. This is especially the case in settings providing out-of-school-time services. For example, in *maisons relais*, working hours are organised around school hours. There are also differences in the perceived value and status of staff. Staff in the non-formal sector struggle to get recognition for the pedagogical work they do – their work seems to be often perceived as just care.

Within the non-formal sector, there are significant differences between working conditions in contracted and non-contracted settings. In the contracted sector, staff salaries are relatively good, and settings do not have difficulties hiring and retaining staff. Wages are fixed as per contracts negotiated by unions, which are adapted every three years and take into account years of experience. The government pays the wage bill in the contracted sector.

In non-contracted settings, salaries are generally lower and are negotiated between the providers and employees at an individual level. There is no collective bargaining as in the contracted sector. There are no regulations for these salaries apart from the legal minimum wage. Small or single-setting non-contracted providers usually have less staff available to carry out administrative tasks and pedagogical reflection or cover for staff in training. Big commercial providers or chains, on the other hand, may have the internal resources to support this.

Differences in working conditions within the non-formal sector are affecting staff retention, particularly in settings for the youngest children

A career in ECEC in Luxembourg is attractive to candidates, as there is significant demand for ECEC staff, and working conditions are relatively advantageous in the formal sector and in non-formal contracted settings. However, retaining staff is a challenge for non-contracted settings in the non-formal sector where working conditions are less advantageous. In particular, non-contracted settings struggle to keep staff that speak Luxembourgish, which is a MENJE requirement (see "The professionalisation of the workforce" section). Given their difficulty in recruiting highly qualified staff, non-contracted settings seem to struggle to align their practices and pedagogies with the ambitious quality requirements and the national curriculum framework for non-formal education. As non-contracted settings are mostly settings serving children aged 0-4 (*crèches*), this might be creating quality gaps across age groups. The quality gap between *maisons relais* and pre-primary settings might also affect the continuity of children's experience of ECEC, given that they transition across sectors multiple times, even in the same day.

Difficulties attracting and retaining staff have implications on the quality of services, especially for small, non-contracted settings. The quality requirements (drafting of the pedagogical concept, consistent use of a logbook, training requirements, implementation of a programme for multilingualism) can be burdensome for small settings, and difficulties filling vacant positions can create challenges for these settings. For example, in some of these settings, staff are not involved in the design of the pedagogical concept, as they do not have time to participate in tasks other than in direct contact with children. Ensuring that the monitoring system does not lead to excessive administrative burden and that quality requirements are proportionate to the capacity and size of settings merit further attention (see Chapter 3).

Part-time work is a source of low wages. Part-time work is common for contracted and non-contracted settings that offer services in the early morning, lunchtime and the end of the day (such as in *maisons relais*) and staff in these settings can be in precarious situations. It may be worth exploring possibilities to find arrangements to improve this situation and reduce turnover rates. One possibility would be to find arrangements for staff with an ISCED 3 qualification to work both in non-formal and formal education settings for children aged 3-4 (*education précoce*). This would allow staff to add up the hours in both sectors, resulting in a full-time contract.

In many countries, the working conditions of staff working with the youngest children are poorer than for staff working with older children (OECD, 2021[1]). In some countries with integrated settings for ECEC for children under the age of 3 and pre-primary education (e.g. Norway), working conditions are more favourable, and the status of the profession is higher (OECD, 2020[10]).

However, Luxembourg aims to maintain its approach (two integrated systems for non-formal and formal education, both spanning across ages) while strengthening quality rather than moving to a fully integrated system. This requires aligning working conditions in each part of the system with staff profiles, roles and responsibilities and providing possibilities for staff to work in various parts of the system and progress in their careers. The gap in staff working conditions and profiles (e.g. qualification) between the non-formal contracted and non-contracted sectors needs to be mitigated, and staff with higher qualifications and good knowledge of the curriculum framework (pedagogical referents, as discussed earlier in this chapter) need to work in both parts of the non-formal sector. This entails collecting and analysing information on the cost of ECEC provision in the non-contracted sector and resources of this sector (e.g. parental fees) to understand why settings offer wages below those of the contracted sector. As wages in the contracted sector are negotiated between employees and employer representatives through collective bargaining, but paid by the government, investigating whether wages have not escalated too much in this part of the sector and are still aligned with staff qualifications and skills could be worthwhile (see Chapter 1). The monitoring system also has a vital role to play in ensuring that public funding translates into high quality in all parts of the sector and that settings in the non-contracted sector face incentives to increase wages so as to retain staff who are needed to meet the quality requirements (see Chapter 3).

Differences in working conditions between formal and non-formal education create fragmentation in the ECEC system

The different working conditions in formal and non-formal education create quality gaps and fragmentation across sectors, which ultimately affects the continuity of children's experiences across settings and levels of education. The existing asymmetries between formal and non-formal staff regarding qualifications, working conditions and status are a barrier to co-operation between the two sectors, affecting staff perceptions and willingness to collaborate.

According to regional officers' reports, staff in the non-formal sector feel that their work is undervalued by society, which can be partly linked to the fact that their salaries are lower than in the formal sector, even for staff with similar qualifications. Another explanation can be the fact that the non-formal sector has only been established fairly recently. For instance, an assistant (with an ISCED Level 3 qualification, *éducateur diplômé*) working in the non-formal sector has lower working conditions than an assistant working alongside teachers in the first year of formal ECEC (*éducation précoce*). In addition, there is a feeling among staff in the non-formal sector that formal sector teachers do not acknowledge their pedagogical work and tend to reduce it to care. Consequently, teachers in the formal sector are often not interested in collaborating in joint projects with staff in the non-formal sector. This is an issue for staff in the non-formal sector, as this collaboration is a requirement for them, which is not the case in formal education.

During the coronavirus (COVID-19) pandemic, the formal and non-formal sectors started collaborating more, as they had to periodically exchange information on children. This experience may be a building block for the future. Another potential model of co-operation across the sectors is the relationship between *maisons relais* and primary schools. Staff working in *maisons relais* have daily contact with their colleagues in formal education since they deliver and pick up children from school, or they sometimes share the same buildings.

To improve transitions across levels, the formal sector should also be encouraged to co-operate with the non-formal sector. As collaboration with the formal sector is part of monitoring in the non-formal sector, there should be inspections looking at the same factors in the formal sector as well. In the longer term, if the qualifications and skills of staff in the non-formal sector increase as recommended in this chapter, the gap in working conditions between the non-formal and formal sectors should also be mitigated.

Plans to review the status of home-based provision can improve quality and working conditions

Home-based providers are highly regulated in Luxembourg. They need to have a diploma in psychosocial, pedagogical, socio-educational or health fields, to have undertaken a number of certified trainings before entering the profession, including on home-based ECEC, to understand and express themselves in at least one of the three official languages, to undertake 20 hours of professional development per year and to develop a project on how they will take care of children. While there are no available data on home-based providers' working conditions, because of their independent status, they might work hours beyond the contracted ones for preparation and reflection on activities and can be exposed to stress related to lack of information and support on administrative issues. They might also struggle to find replacements for taking take time off for sickness or vacation, also generating stress.

There are ongoing discussions in the sector regarding changing the status of home-based providers to improve their working conditions and the quality of their services. An approach to foster links and activities between home-based providers and centre-based settings is also under consideration. The government is currently conducting a benchmark study to investigate the situation in other European countries.

If the status of home-based providers is changed, care needs to be taken to ensure that changes allow them to concentrate on the pedagogical work and be in closer contact with the offer for quality support and professional development trainings. Integrating home-based providers into centre-based structures can help raise their perceived value to the same level as centre-based settings. With this mixed approach, however, it will be important to respect the specificity of home-based providers and the family-based model that they offer, as many parents look for this type of environment for their children. It will also be important that the new arrangement provides parents with the flexibility they may seek with home-based provision, such as flexible opening hours. This can include better integrating home-based provision with centre-based provision and ensuring smooth transitions between the two.

References

Aboagye, M. et al. (2020), "Managing conflictual teacher-child relationship in pre-schools: A preliminary test of the job resources buffering-effect hypothesis in an emerging economy", *Children and Youth Services Review*, Vol. 118. [28]

Aboagye, M. et al. (2020), "Finding something good in the bad: The curvilinear emotional demand-conflict teacher-child relationship link", *Early Child Development and Care*, pp. 1-18. [29]

Ansari, A. et al. (2020), "Preschool teachers' emotional exhaustion in relation to classroom instruction and teacher-child interactions", *Early Education and Development*, Vol. 33/1, pp. 1-14, http://dx.doi.org/10.1080/10409289.2020.1848301. [27]

Balduzzi, L. and A. Lazzari (2015), "Mentoring practices in workplace-based professional preparation: A critical analysis of policy developments in the Italian context", *Early Years*, Vol. 35/2, pp. 124-138. [7]

Boeskens, L., D. Nusche and M. Yurita (2020), "Policies to support teachers' continuing professional learning: A conceptual framework and mapping of OECD data", *OECD Education Working Papers*, No. 235, OECD Publishing, Paris, https://dx.doi.org/10.1787/247b7c4d-en. [19]

Cassidy, D. et al. (2017), "Teacher work environments are toddler learning environments: Teacher professional well-being, classroom emotional support, and toddlers' emotional expressions and behaviours", *Early Child Development and Care*, Vol. 187/11, pp. 1666-1678, http://dx.doi.org/10.1080/03004430.2016.1180516. [25]

Cazes, S., A. Hijzen and A. Saint-Martin (2015), "Measuring and Assessing Job Quality: The OECD Job Quality Framework", *OECD Social, Employment and Migration Working Papers*, No. 174, OECD Publishing, Paris, https://dx.doi.org/10.1787/5jrp02kjw1mr-en. [24]

Chen, S., B. Phillips and B. Izci (2018), "Teacher–child relational conflict in Head Start – Exploring the roles of child behaviour, teacher stress, and bias, and classroom environment", *Early Child Development and Care*, Vol. 190/8, pp. 1174-1186. [30]

Douglass, A. (2019), "Leadership for quality early childhood education and care", *OECD Education Working Papers*, No. 211, OECD Publishing, Paris, https://doi.org/10.1787/6e563bae-en. [20]

Eckhardt, A. and F. Egert (2020), "Predictors for the quality of family child care: A meta-analysis", *Children and Youth Services Review*, Vol. 116. [12]

Egert, F., V. Dederer and R. Fukkink (2020), "The impact of in-service professional development on the quality of teacher-child interactions in early education and care: A meta-analysis", *Educational Research Review*, Vol. 29. [13]

Flämig, K., A. König and N. Spiekermann (2015), "Potentials, dissonances and reform initiatives in field-based learning and mentoring practices in the early childhood sector in Germany", *Early Years*, Vol. 35/2, pp. 211-226. [8]

Hamre, B., A. Partee and C. Mulcahy (2017), "Enhancing the impact of professional development in the context of preschool expansion", *AERA Open*, Vol. 3/4, https://doi.org/10.1177/2332858417733686. [11]

Hu, B. et al. (2017), "Are structural quality indicators associated with preschool process quality in China? An exploration of threshold effects", *Early Childhood Research Quarterly*, Vol. 40, pp. 163-173, http://dx.doi.org/10.1016/j.ecresq.2017.03.006. [26]

Kaarby, K. and I. Lindboe (2016), "The workplace as learning environment in early childhood teacher education: An investigation of work-based education", *Higher Education Pedagogies*, Vol. 1/1, pp. 106-120. [9]

Lin, Y. and K. Magnusson (2018), "Classroom quality and children's academic skills in child care centers: Understanding the role of teacher qualifications", *Early Childhood Research Quarterly*, Vol. Vol. 42, pp. 215-227,, http://dx.doi.org/10.1016/j.ecresq.2017.1. [4]

Manning, M. et al. (2017), "The relationship between teacher qualification and the quality of the early childhood education and care environment", *Campbell Systematic Reviews*, Vol. 1, pp. 1-82, http://dx.doi.org/10.4073/csr.2017.1. [3]

Markussen-Brown, J. et al. (2017), "The effects of language-and literacy-focused professional development on early educators and children: A best-evidence meta-analysis", *Early Childhood Research Quarterly*, Vol. 38, pp. 97-115. [14]

OECD (2021), *Starting Strong VI: Supporting Meaningful Interactions in Early Childhood Education and Care*, Starting Strong, OECD Publishing, Paris, https://dx.doi.org/10.1787/f47a06ae-en. [1]

OECD (2020), *Building a High-Quality Early Childhood Education and Care Workforce: Further Results from the Starting Strong Survey 2018*, TALIS, OECD Publishing, Paris, https://dx.doi.org/10.1787/b90bba3d-en. [10]

OECD (2020), *Building a High-Quality Early Childhood Education and Care Workforce: Further Results from the Starting Strong Survey 2018*, TALIS, OECD Publishing, Paris, https://dx.doi.org/10.1787/b90bba3d-en. [21]

OECD (2020), *Education at a Glance 2020: OECD Indicators*, OECD Publishing, Paris, https://dx.doi.org/10.1787/69096873-en. [31]

OECD (2019), *Providing Quality Early Childhood Education and Care: Results from the Starting Strong Survey 2018*, TALIS, OECD Publishing, Paris, https://dx.doi.org/10.1787/301005d1-en. [5]

OECD (2019), *Working and Learning Together: Rethinking Human Resource Policies for Schools*, OECD Reviews of School Resources, OECD Publishing, Paris, https://dx.doi.org/10.1787/b7aaf050-en. [22]

OECD (2018), *Engaging Young Children: Lessons from Research about Quality in Early Childhood Education and Care*, Starting Strong, OECD Publishing, Paris, https://dx.doi.org/10.1787/9789264085145-en. [2]

OECD (2015), *Schooling Redesigned: Towards Innovative Learning Systems*, Educational Research and Innovation, OECD Publishing, Paris, https://doi.org/10.1787/9789264245914-en. [23]

Peleman, B. et al. (2018), "Continuous professional development and ECEC quality: Findings from a European systematic literature review", *European Journal of Education*, Vol. 53/1, pp. 9-22. [16]

Sandilos, L. et al. (2018), "Does professional development reduce the influence of teacher stress on teacher-child interactions in pre-kindergarten classrooms?", *Early Childhood Research Quarterly*, Vol. 42, pp. 280-290. [17]

Totenhagen, C. et al. (2015), "Retaining early childhood education workers: A review of the empirical literature", *Journal of Research in Childhood Education*, Vol. 30/4, pp. 585-599, http://dx.doi.org/10.1080/02568543.2016.1214652. [18]

von Suchodoletz, A. et al. (2017), *"Associations among quality indicators in early childhood education and care (ECEC) and relations with child development and learning: A meta-analysis"*, Internal document, OECD, Paris. [6]

Werner, C. et al. (2016), "Do intervention programs in child care promote the quality of caregiver-child interactions? A meta-analysis of randomized controlled trials", *Prevention Science*, Vol. 17/2, pp. 259-273. [15]

3 Quality assurance and improvement in the non-formal early childhood education and care sector in Luxembourg

This chapter discusses Luxembourg's main strengths and challenges in developing a system for quality assurance and improvement that best support the non-formal early childhood education and care sector. It describes governance and responsibilities in monitoring quality, monitoring processes and tools, and the consequences and use of monitoring results to promote improvement, particularly on non-formal education.

Introduction

Governments worldwide have increased their investments in early childhood education and care (ECEC) to improve the accessibility and quality of ECEC services, both of which are needed for ECEC services to deliver the benefits demonstrated by rigorous research evidence (OECD, 2015[1]; 2018[2]; 2021[3]). To ensure high quality, countries are moving towards developing a highly structured, professionalised and regulated ECEC system. Data and monitoring are important drivers of quality and essential parts of quality assurance systems. They help demonstrate facts and trends, thus producing evidence on equitable access to ECEC, whether minimum standards of quality are met, whether ECEC settings offer children experiences that support their development and well-being and whether measures are in place to achieve improvements (OECD, 2015[1]; 2018[2]; 2021[3]; EC/EACEA/Eurydice, 2019[4]). Supporting such developments, research has shown that the presence and efficiency of regulation and data collection mechanisms across countries are associated with better educational outcomes for children (Pascal et al., 2013[5]).

Across countries, the levels of regulation and data collection vary. More variation has been observed, particularly for the younger age group in ECEC and home-based providers. Some countries are increasing their efforts to strengthen quality assurance mechanisms in those areas (EC/EACEA/Eurydice, 2019[4]). In addition, countries increasingly focus on developing monitoring systems that seek to enhance process quality as well as structural quality. This is the result of a consensus that structural quality aspects (those addressing space, materials, staff-to-child ratios, group sizes, levels of staff qualification and curriculum frameworks) are closely linked to the conditions for children in ECEC to experience good quality interactions (process quality), which are the main drivers of their development (Melhuish et al., 2015[6]; OECD, 2021[3]; Shuey and Kankaras, 2018[7]).

These trends can also be observed in the ECEC sector in Luxembourg. Following the introduction of the ECEC subsidy funding scheme (chèque-service accueil, CSA) in 2009 to increase the accessibility of ECEC in the non-formal sector, services have seen a rapid expansion and increased participation of young children (under age 3) in ECEC, particularly through the vast growth of a private-for-profit sector. In addition to the expansion of provision, Luxembourg also introduced further measures in the development and assurance of quality in the non-formal education sector. These measures cover all types of non-formal providers and all age groups and include a focus on structural and process quality (Achten and Bodeving, 2017[8]; Luxembourg Ministry of Education, Children and Youth, 2020[9]).

Monitoring quality and measuring effectiveness are challenging tasks that require co-ordinated and strategic processes as well as the collection of reliable data (OECD, 2015[1]). Countries employ many different approaches to ensure that monitoring results and data can inform planning, contribute to more efficient resource allocation, and lead to improved programme quality and child outcomes (OECD, 2018[2]). This chapter will discuss the strengths and challenges in Luxembourg's current policy and practice, and current developments that are underway with a focus on non-formal education, in relation to the following areas:

- governance and responsibilities in monitoring quality, considering differences across monitoring areas and purposes of monitoring
- monitoring processes, including a focus on the preparation of evaluators, and the frameworks and tools in place to support monitoring
- the consequences and use of monitoring results.

The chapter also makes recommendations for ongoing and future policy developments, as summarised in Box 3.1.

Recommendations for the whole ECEC sector

Governance of quality assurance and monitoring

- Continue to locate all monitoring activity for non-formal and formal education within the Ministry of Education, Children and Youth because a single ministry supports a coherent accountability and improvement system.

- Bring together knowledge on ECEC quality across the formal and non-formal sectors to build collaboration and create connections for children and families.

- Prioritise work on the centrally organised, systematic collection of information on the sufficiency of ECEC provision, characteristics of children and families participating in ECEC and the diversity of the workforce, including the language profiles of children, families and staff.

Recommendations for non-formal education

Governance and responsibilities for quality assurance

- Strengthen the channels through which intelligence on quality gathered during visits from the two monitoring bodies (the *Direction générale du secteur enfance* and the *Service national de la jeunesse)* can be used to improve quality, including by reviewing funding allocations as well as creating a feedback loop on pre-service and in-service workforce training.

- Improve communication of the new responsibilities of the two bodies in their roles of control versus support to enhance the work of both. Act on several fronts to enhance the capacities of regional officers to support quality improvement in the sector (e.g. better preparedness for their role, more time to focus on quality improvement and well-identified tools).

Monitoring processes and tools

- Broaden the sources of information on quality available to regional officers during their visits. Engage ECEC staff, parents and children in monitoring visits (possibly mounting parent surveys in advance of the visit) to broaden and deepen the knowledge of process quality.

- Develop systematic observations of staff interactions with children as well as children's interactions with one another and introduce observational monitoring tools to assess process quality. The framework against which process quality would be assessed requires a clear focus on interactions that foster children's development along the goals of the curriculum framework, such as experiences to foster the development of socio-emotional skills, emotional resilience, or respect for diversity.

- Introduce recommendations for ECEC staff to document children's engagement in learning experiences to aid identification of children's needs and interests, and communicate this to parents and schools for children enrolled in formal education. Aspects that might be useful to document are child experiences that encourage the development of 21st-century skills (e.g. collaboration, creativity and self-regulation).

- Offer further training for regional officers on making recommendations for improvement and supporting providers to draw up their own self-improvement plans.

- Expand the selection and/or training requirements of regional officers to include specialisation in early childhood and ideally work experience in ECEC provision.

- Require providers to have a comprehensive complaint management process and develop a more formal system for service users to have complaints reviewed by regional officers.

The consequences and use of monitoring results

- Review the steps available to put in place when a provider consistently falls short of expected quality levels. Develop and use self-improvement plans to follow up on implementing improvement strategies and identify persistent low-quality providers. Ensure that improvement strategies are acted upon by providers, implemented in a timely manner and reviewed by regional officers.

- Encourage centre leaders to share the results of external monitoring with ECEC staff members (perhaps in condensed form) and involve staff in designing improvement plans. Strengthen the capacity of the staff to undertake self-evaluation, in improvement planning in their own provision (e.g. through specific training). Ensure the results of self-evaluation are reviewed during inspections.

- Consider using the monitoring results to feed into risk-based, proportionate approach to monitoring visit programming, which will help channel monitoring resources, for example, by introducing flexibility in the frequency of monitoring visits to tailor inspection according to the needs of providers.

- Investigate better ways to channel information about gaps in process quality to the training institutions so that monitoring feeds directly into future in-service and pre-service training.

- Introduce a requirement to publish (for example, on a parent portal or through formal communication to a structure's "parent committee") condensed information on the monitoring results (e.g. improvement plans and progress towards achieving goals).

- Use data to analyse costs for ECEC providers in relation to subsidies and parent fees to understand if tighter mechanisms need to be developed to ensure that resources are targeted efficiently to ensure quality and equity.
  - Use this analysis also to clarify if there is a need to review public funding in the contracted and non-contracted sectors or if targeted funding should be allocated to certain providers based on the characteristics of participating children.
  - Use resulting data to identify patterns of ECEC participation among diverse families, including the use of home-based versus centre-based ECEC, enrolment in contracted versus non-contracted settings, and reasons for forgoing participation in settings for children aged 3-4 (*éducation précoce*).

Governance and responsibilities for quality assurance in the ECEC sector

Context

Countries employ different monitoring systems, which can be indicative of different systems of provision for different age groups and reflect levels of centralisation or decentralisation of governance and supervision (EC/EACEA/Eurydice, 2019[10]). The scope of external monitoring is often related to the type of body responsible for the external evaluation of settings (EC/EACEA/Eurydice, 2019[4]).

In Luxembourg, the provision of ECEC is split between the non-formal sector providing ECEC for children until age 3 or 4, and the formal sector providing ECEC for children over 3, and in doing so working in shared responsibility with the non-formal sector providing for children until age 12 during out-of-school time. National quality assurance arrangements for ECEC, including licensing, regulation, inspection and quality assurance, exist for all types of ECEC provision, including formal and non-formal education providers, and centre-based as well as home-based provision.

Across both the non-formal and formal sectors, the education authority has the main responsibility for governing ECEC, and separate national bodies under the Ministry of Education, Children and Youth (MENJE) are in charge of funding, regulating, organising and supervising monitoring. A split pattern between different bodies responsible for regulatory inspection and process quality can be observed in several countries in Europe. Similar to Luxembourg, separate inspectorates also exist at the national level in several countries (including Ireland, Wales [United Kingdom] and Scotland [United Kingdom]) (EC/EACEA/Eurydice, 2019[4]; OECD, 2021[3]). This split pattern can result from an introduction of process quality monitoring well after inspection processes for structural quality were established earlier.

In Luxembourg, separation of monitoring across different divisions reflects the split between the formal and non-formal sectors, as well as the historically separate introduction of structural versus process quality monitoring processes over time, with currently increasing efforts to separate inspection roles of controlling from quality improvement roles.

The provision of non-formal ECEC is regulated by the ASFT Act (*Loi du 8 septembre 1998 réglant les relations entre l'Etat et les organismes oeuvrant dans les domaines social, familial et thérapeutique*), which defines formal requirements for ECEC providers as well as safety regulations. Requirements concerning structural quality (child-staff ratio, group sizes, infrastructure, etc.) are regulated by a Grand-Ducal Ordonnance (*Règlement grand-ducal modifié du 14 novembre 2013 concernant l'agrément à accorder aux gestionnaires de services d'éducation et d'accueil pour enfants*). Since 2007, a law has been in place to regulate the provision of home-based care, with a focus on structural quality aspects such as space, and number of children in care, and the education and training of childminders (*Loi du 30 novembre 2007 portant réglementation de l'activité d'assistance parentale*) (Achten and Bodeving, 2017[8]). Settings must meet those standards to achieve and maintain licensing, which is statutory for all providers (SNJ, 2021[11]).

Measures for process quality are anchored in the Youth Acts from 2008 (*Loi sur la jeunesse*) and its modification from 2016. Until 2016, non-formal education settings had no obligations in terms of their process quality (SNJ, 2021[11]). In Luxembourg, the quality assurance system in non-formal education is linked to the ECEC subsidy funding scheme, and those settings that wish to be recognised under the subsidy funding scheme by the Ministry of Education, Children and Youth (which is nearly all providers) must meet a number of requirements. These include implementing the national curriculum – the National Reference Framework on the Non-formal Education of Children and Youth (*Cadre de référence national sur l'éducation non formelle des enfants et des jeunes*) and (for children aged 1-4) implementing the multilingual education programme, meeting obligations on continuous professional development, and accepting external evaluations through regular monitoring visits.

In the non-formal sector, there is a split in quality monitoring responsibilities and functions between two divisions, both under MENJE. Agents (or inspectors) under the Department for Children (*Direction générale du secteur de l'enfance*) are in charge of licensing and maintaining and managing the national register, checking eligibility for the ECEC subsidy funding scheme, and monitoring for accountability purposes, with a stronger focus on structural quality aspects and compliance with regulatory standards (Figure 3.1). On the other hand, regional officers (*agents régionaux*) working under the National Youth Service (*Service national de la jeunesse*, SNJ) have a strong mission to monitor process quality and focus on quality improvement. Their monitoring body is relatively new, having been introduced in 2017.

The system with two separate bodies in charge of monitoring procedures requires communication channels between the two divisions: 1) SNJ regional officers use information from structural monitoring and inspection to check whether conditions are set for the curriculum requirements (i.e. level of qualifications for multilingual programmes); and 2) SNJ regional officers who visit settings more frequently are in communication with agents under the Department for Children and can report on other issues in addition to their core mission if weaknesses or non-compliance is observed during their monitoring process. This role is seen as important for quality improvement, inasmuch as 3) to support the development of quality standards, regional officers also collaborate with other divisions and external institutions (e.g. the

SNJ's Innovation Division, the multilingual programme team, the University of Luxembourg and the Agence Dageselteren).

Figure 3.1. Governance of quality assurance and improvement support in ECEC in the non-formal sector in Luxembourg

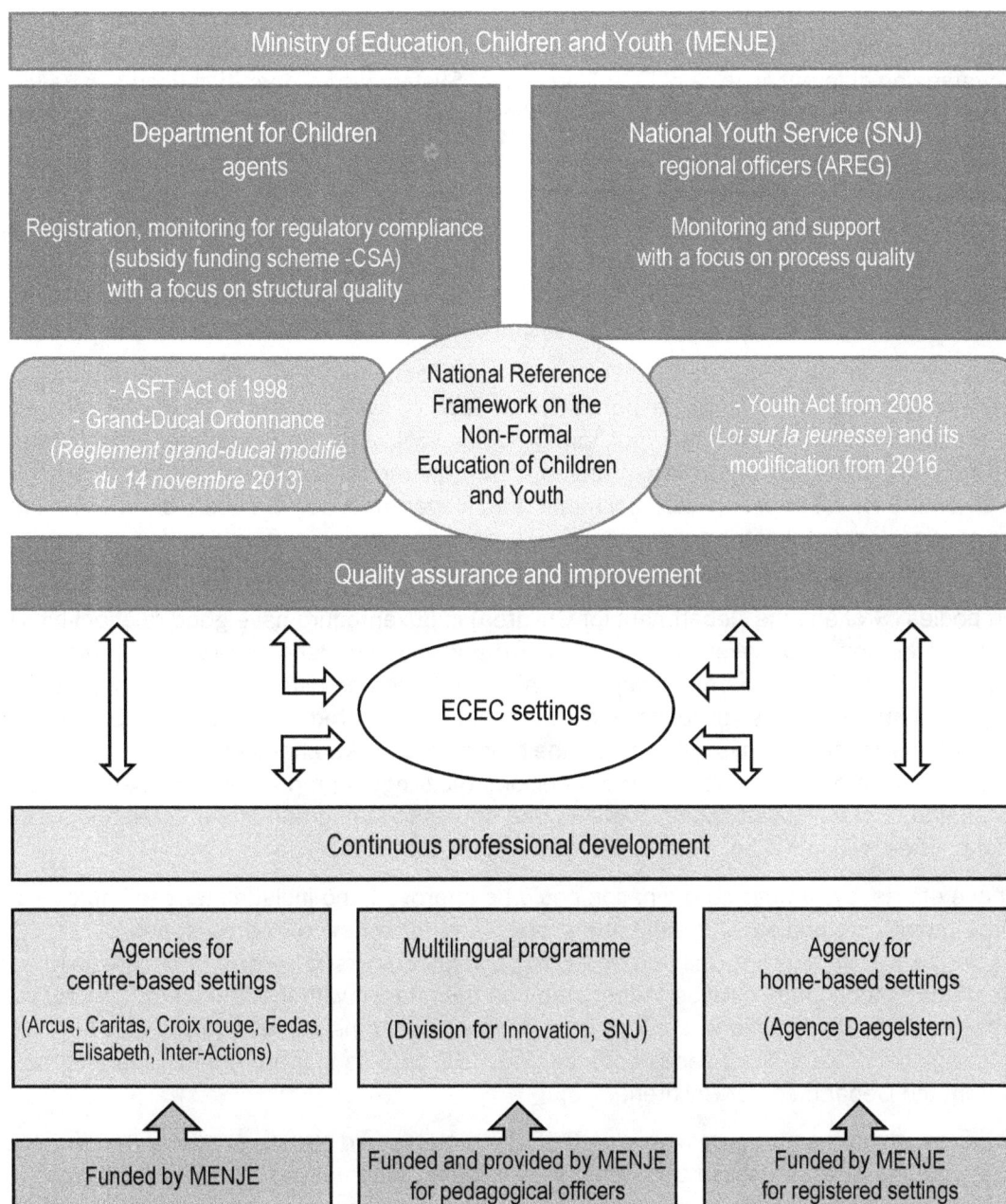

Source: Authors' own elaboration, based on SNJ (2021[11]), *Quality Beyond Regulations in Early Childhood Education and Care (ECEC): Country Background Report of Luxembourg*, Service national de la jeunesse.

In the formal ECEC sector, regional directors are responsible for the pedagogical and administrative management of schools. The country is divided into 15 regions under one minister's authority and is managed by one director, assisted by two to four deputy directors. They are in charge of pedagogical monitoring as well as the co-ordination in the management of children with special educational needs and disabilities.

Co-ordination between agencies with roles for non-formal education could be further improved

In Luxembourg, the fact that different ECEC monitoring responsibilities are under one single authority of MENJE provides a structure set up to strengthen communication and collaboration between different divisions overseeing different aspects of ECEC provision. Systematic co-operation occurs at various levels (e.g. regional officers exchange with the Department for Children on issues and questions related to specific ECEC settings).

For non-formal education, co-ordination channels exist between the SNJ *Développement de la qualité* division and other SNJ divisions or MENJE departments (e.g. communication with the Department for Children, with the further training co-ordination team of SNJ, with the team of the multilingual programme, or with the agency for home-based ECEC) to ensure that the results of monitoring reports lead to necessary actions that address, for example, staff training in centre-based and home-based provision.

Until recently, communication channels between regional officers from SNJ and agents of the Department for Children were mainly informal. In response to the lack of systematic exchanges at this level, new exchange procedures between the two monitoring bodies (SNJ and the Department for Children) were introduced recently, and their roles were clarified. The new model was implemented in autumn 2021. The new co-ordination efforts between SNJ and the Department for Children should be sustained. Monitoring needs to ensure that the actions taken in response to new co-ordination efforts can guide further improvements across the sector.

Monitoring bodies (SNJ and the Department for Children) in Luxembourg have good relationships with the University of Luxembourg (*Université du Luxembourg*) and with independent research centres. They are regularly invited to collaborate in organising national conferences on different aspects of process quality (SNJ, 2021[11]). Through regular dialogue and government-sponsored, specific research studies, those responsible for the monitoring systems review their work and make changes when appropriate. As an example of the use of external research, the ambitious multilingual programme has been the subject of external research, a practice that should continue and serves to strengthen one of Luxembourg's flagship educational policies, which will be of interest to many other countries.

Despite these efforts, systematic co-ordination could be improved and include steps to improve data flow between the monitoring bodies. Currently, there are plans for a new digital database on ECEC, which would enable the Department for Children and SNJ regional officers to enter and access information on the results of their monitoring activities. A first step has been taken with the launch of the new version of the database, *Banque de données assurance qualité*, which concerns process quality. It is mainly used by SNJ and its regional officers, but it sends updates on ECEC centres that are not fulfilling their obligations to agents from the Department for Children.

A second project concerns a new database on ECEC structures and structural quality that MENJE would use. Data exchange between these two databases is being automatised to avoid duplication of work. There will be requirements for providers to enter information on this new second digital platform and upload documentation for inspectors from the Department for Children to check. The aim is to ensure that the Department for Children has access to and can check up-to-date information on settings. It is also hoped that this digital platform will improve transparency, streamline and rationalise staff activities in settings, as well as help external evaluators involved in the monitoring process.

The digital ECEC database should be used so that information on quality identified during regional officers' visits can be linked to specific aspects of enrolment, staff training and funding. However, care will have to be taken to ensure that arrangements for entering, sharing and monitoring this information do not become too complex, nor take additional time away from staff focusing on children's experiences. This is particularly important for small, non-formal, centre-based settings in Luxembourg, as well as home-based providers – both low in resources to deal with growing external and administrative demands and requirements.

Clarifying the roles of the two monitoring agencies for non-formal ECEC can enhance the work of both and strengthen the mechanisms to support quality improvement

Luxembourg increasingly emphasises the role of its regional officers to support quality improvement. It is striving for a clearer separation between monitoring purposes of controlling versus purposes of quality improvement, anchored in the separate responsibilities of agents from the Department for Children and regional officers from SNJ. Despite these efforts, however, there have been certain overlaps in their roles, causing some tensions, particularly in relation to the roles of regional officers, which are mainly in support but nevertheless include some purpose of control. First, regional officers inform agents under the Department for Children if non-compliance with regulations is observed during their visits. Second, they are one point of contact for complaints and forward them to responsible agents at the Department for Children where necessary (Achten and Bodeving, 2017[8]). The complaint office at the Department for Children can also be contacted directly by parents and professionals. Until the end of 2021, regional officers also checked compliance with professional development requirements (on number of hours). Recently there were dialogues between the two departments regarding the responsibilities. From the beginning of 2022, regional officers were released from their duty to check compliance with professional development requirements. It is now up to the ECEC centre managers to ensure that their staff fulfils legal requirements.

Releasing regional officers from duties to monitor compliance will help reduce some tensions. However, if the control function of regional officers is further reduced, MENJE will need to further consider the role of its agents (Department for Children) in monitoring compliance with regulations. The frequency of visits carried out by agents from the Department for Children is significantly lower than for regional officers, and mechanisms may have to be put in place to ensure the information on structural aspects of quality of provision is always up to date and regularly monitored. The introduction of the new digital database, as outlined above, might support this process.

In the short and long terms, bringing together knowledge on ECEC quality across the formal and non-formal sectors can build collaboration and create connections for children and families

The strength of the Luxembourg ECEC system is that both formal and non-formal provision are under one authority, MENJE, and therefore well placed to ensure that ECEC services in both sectors complement each other, and *in combination,* provide children (and families) with the range of experiences best suited to support child development and well-being. Luxembourg's introduction of a national curriculum framework for the non-formal sector (including ECEC) aligned with the formal ECEC sector curriculum is an important step in this direction. What connects the frameworks is the definition of "fields of action" – the range of experiences to be offered to children to support their well-being and learning holistically. At the same time, there are important intended differences between the two sectors. This relates to pedagogical principals and approaches, which reflect what is specific to the provision of ECEC in each sector.

Thus, the ECEC system in Luxembourg sets itself the challenging task of ensuring connectedness while preserving each sector's specific focus and intentions. The OECD review team heard about certain gaps in the shared understanding between the two sectors, suggesting that more could be done to bring together the knowledge and expertise on the provision of quality (including strengths and challenges) established in both the non-formal and formal sectors. Channels of communication between the two sectors should be strengthened. In particular, this should include a focus on learning and sharing about pedagogical and multilingual approaches that should facilitate planning across sectors that is in the best interests of the child (see Chapter 1).

Meeting demand and ensuring affordable access to ECEC require ongoing data collection

Participation rates have to be assessed in relation to the sufficiency of ECEC provision. Demand is higher than supply in many countries for the younger age group (children under 3), and shortages can be higher in some regions (e.g. rural areas) (OECD, 2020[12]). In combination with other barriers to participation, the shortage of places can mean that those families and children who might benefit most from ECEC participation are more likely to miss out.

Costs to parents is a main barrier to ECEC participation, particularly for low-income families. A real strength of the ECEC system in Luxembourg is unconditional free access up to 20 hours per week for all children aged 1-4 in centre-based settings; targeted entitlements for (additional) free hours for more disadvantaged populations; and subsidised hours depending on parents' income (see Chapter 1). Importantly, these measures apply to children from ages 1-4 and across all types of provision apart from the free 20 hours per week for centre-based settings. Yet, ECEC in Luxembourg does not come without parental costs. These are related to hours beyond the free offer, most notably before children enter the formal schooling sector. In Luxembourg, there are no regulations regarding parental costs in the non-contracted sector, which is the main sector providing for children under the age of 3. Moreover, children enrolled in home-based settings do not benefit from the 20 free hours, although they are covered by the subsidy funding system.

In addition, parental leave policies in Luxembourg mean that there can be a gap between when parental leave ends and the age of 1, which is when free access to ECEC starts (under the ECEC subsidy funding system). Gaps could affect low-income families disproportionally since full-time parental leave lasts four to six months, leaving ECEC costs up to parents for the remaining six to eight months. In addition, some families (in lower paid employment in particular) may have less flexibility to take on part-time parental leave entitlements to stretch parental leave to cover for more months, for example, up to age 1.

Collecting information on the uptake of home-based services and centre-based services in both the contracted and non-contracted sectors and linking this information to existing data on the fees charged by non-contracted settings would enable the government in Luxembourg to better understand the successes and limitations of the current approach to free and subsidised ECEC (see Chapter 1).

Systematic data collection on ECEC in Luxembourg is expanding and can be further strengthened

The evaluation of policies that ensure accessibility and quality of ECEC services requires availability of information on what is effective, in which context and for whom. In terms of access, crucial information includes data on participation rates in relation to the sufficiency of provision, or parental costs, linked to the types of providers and demographics of users. In Luxembourg, and regarding accessibility and quality of non-formal ECEC provision, aspects that need consideration are:

- **The diversity of families and children participating in ECEC**. In Luxembourg, such diversity is immense in relation to children's language backgrounds as well as parental values and expectations concerning ECEC. While language barriers, knowledge of procedures, or differences in values and beliefs can create barriers to participation (Eurofound, 2012[13]), these factors can also lead families with different background characteristics to choose or find access to different types of ECEC providers. This can cause a division between different types of providers and risk segregation across ECEC services. Segregation can impact the degree of social mix that has been found to be beneficial to children's development, and it can challenge those providers who serve those children and families with more disadvantages or needs (de Haan et al., 2013[14]; Early et al., 2010[15]; Kuger and Kluczniok, 2008[16]).

- **The diversity of the workforce**. With its diverse workforce, trained in different countries with different traditions (including Belgium, France and Germany), Luxembourg's challenge is the diversity of initial training programmes completed by their workforce. Systematic collection of information on the workforce needs to include a focus on this issue. Importantly, working conditions also vary across different types of providers in Luxembourg, resulting in disparities of staff with different profiles between the private sector and the contracted sector in particular and issues with staff retention. These are all important issues to monitor.

- **The language profiles of users and the workforce in ECEC**. The multilingual education programme is an important element of Luxembourg's ECEC offer. Children in ECEC are to be exposed to Luxembourgish and French, and to be encouraged to express themselves in their home languages. Requirements on language competencies of the workforce are in place, but (related to the diversity of the workforce and the concentration of staff who commute across borders to work in certain regions and types of ECEC providers in Luxembourg) there are difficulties in meeting those requirements. To address language gaps and ensure that requirements can be met, systematic collection of information on children, families and staff should focus on their language profiles.

- **Providers outside the ECEC subsidy funding system**. The quality assurance system in Luxembourg is comprehensive, and regulations that have been put in place include children under the age of 3 and home-based providers. However, the quality assurance system in Luxembourg is linked to the ECEC subsidy funding scheme. Thus, while mandatory for most centres and providers, those not relying on government funding in Luxembourg can work outside the quality assurance system. While the OECD review team heard that the percentage of centres and providers outside the subsidy funding scheme is very low, it would be important to identify those that are and introduce measures to better understand the quality of provision, resources and needs of children and families for those providers.

While Luxembourg collects general data on children's participation rates at different ages (see, for example, EC/EACEA/Eurydice (2019[10])), there is no central systematic collection of information on those who use non-formal ECEC; the demographics of the workforce in the sector; the demand and sufficiency of provision; or working conditions. To support policy development that ensures the accessibility of services and addresses those factors that may impact the quality services can offer (e.g. retention issues, differences in the profile of the workforce across types of providers), the Ministry of Education, Children and Youth should prioritise putting into place a centrally organised, systematic collection of information on: 1) the background characteristics of families accessing different types of ECEC; 2) parental costs across different types of provision; 3) the demand and supply for ECEC places; 4) the socio-demographic profile of the workforce and their educational qualifications, further training, recruitment and retention; and their pay, working hours and work conditions. Attention will need to be paid to examining this information in relation to different types of ECEC providers and quality indicators.

The following sections of this chapter cover non-formal education only.

Monitoring processes and tools

Context

For all types of non-formal ECEC providers in Luxembourg, agents from the Department for Children are responsible for monitoring the following issues as part of the control of structural quality: staff-child ratios, staff qualifications, indoor and outdoor premises, safety regulations and health and/or hygiene regulations (the latter are additionally controlled by the *Inspection du Travail et des Mines* [ITM] and/or the Ministry of Health) (SNJ, 2021[11]). Following licensing, agents conduct monitoring visits every two or three years, and visits can happen unannounced.

Monitoring for process quality in Luxembourg includes a focus on pedagogy and curriculum framework implementation. Like many other countries, Luxembourg employs external evaluation practices and tools to monitor aspects of process quality. In addition, self-evaluation is a mandatory requirement for those ECEC providers under the ECEC subsidy funding scheme.

The national curriculum framework is the point of orientation for regional officers from SNJ, and the written pedagogical concept plays an important role in monitoring processes. In their monitoring role, regional officers check that pedagogical concepts and those approaches to practices planned by each setting are aligned with the curriculum framework. Regional officers visit settings one to two times per year and give settings two weeks' written notice of their visit. Regional officers are expected to work closely with each setting assigned to them. Each regional officer has up to 40 settings to monitor. Reflection is initiated during, and following visits, and feedback is provided to leaders/managers of ECEC settings. The regional officers follow guidelines during their visits and when drafting their reports.

Monitoring quality does not have a positive impact per se; the procedures and tools for monitoring need to be aligned with intended purposes and implementation strategies (OECD, 2015[1]). With a focus on providing support for quality improvement, regional officers in charge of process quality have to collect reliable, relevant, and accurate information to help managers and leaders in ECEC settings make decisions on how best to improve their service. To collect this information, regional officers visit the setting, stay for three to four hours, and focus on three methods: the analysis of internal documents, an open dialogue with the leader of the setting and a check of the premises. During their visit, regional officers mainly interact with the leader, but if there are opportunities, they also interact (briefly) with some staff members or some of the children.

Centre-based ECEC settings have to provide the following internal documents for review by the regional officers: the pedagogical concept and the logbook (or the programme of activities for home-based providers) (Achten and Bodeving, 2017[8]; SNJ, 2021[11]). The pedagogical concept, which needs approval for a three-year period by the Ministry after an in-depth examination by SNJ, includes a pedagogical section, describing the objectives and fundamental pedagogical principles at the local or regional level, self-assessment measures, a definition of areas for which pedagogical quality assurance projects are developed and a continuing professional development plan for the staff. Settings are required by law to make their concepts public, and this is seen as a mechanism that enables parents to compare settings in terms of pedagogical quality (Achten and Bodeving, 2017[8]). The logbook (*journal de bord*) contains the regular (daily or weekly) written descriptions of the functions and the assignment of tasks within each setting, the work regulations of the setting, a list of daily activities with the children and an overview of the staff's participation in continuing professional development (Achten and Bodeving, 2017[8]). Similarly, providers of home-based ECEC have to put together an establishment project, an activity report, and meet compulsory continuing training requirements (Luxembourg Ministry of Education, Children and Youth, 2020[9]).

The analysis of these documents, together with a conversation with the leader, aims to investigate pedagogical orientation and pedagogical practice and whether there is alignment with the national curriculum framework and the multilingual programme. Regional officers are trained to carry out exchanges with the leader of the setting, which focus on the curriculum frameworks' seven areas of action, collaboration with parents and local networks, and management and staff collaboration. Their task is to address the following questions: How are the objectives implemented in daily practice? What activities or projects contribute to achieving these? What attitudes and pedagogical approaches are beneficial? To ensure the setting leader's perspective is captured well, questions are deliberately worded as open questions (Achten and Bodeving, 2017[8]).

Regional officers also carry out a check of the premises, which mainly focuses on the quality of the physical environment: how spaces, furniture, equipment and play and learning materials are organised to facilitate experiences in all curriculum areas that nurture development and support recreational activities and rest. Children and staff are not necessarily present during this observational walk through the setting. However, if they are, regional officers also take notice of children's engagement and the pedagogical practice they observe. Thus, the external evaluation focuses on the implementation of the curriculum – mainly evaluating the alignment with its principles and addressing the areas of action in the planning of daily interaction with children.

SNJ's revision plans currently focus on a new framework document to provide a clearer structure for how regional officers should provide their evaluation reports. Currently, the reports are very descriptive, and the intention is to include an evaluation of the strengths and weaknesses of the quality of provision in different areas, all linked to the curriculum framework. New guidelines to better support regional officers in making judgements on quality aspects have been developed, and implementation started at the end of 2021. The guidelines include pedagogical approaches, environment and materials, staff-child interactions, interactions with parents, and the quality of the management. Indicators are being developed for each area to help regional officers in their evaluation and to better ensure coherence. The indicators have been grouped into six "quality dimensions" (quality of staff, quality of the infrastructure and the equipment, quality of the interaction with the children, quality of the pedagogical offer, quality of the relations with parents, quality of management). The aim is not to provide a quantitative judgement of the quality of a setting but to identify ways to promote quality at the setting level, as well as to understand how the sector as a whole is developing and where resources and support need to be improved.

Staff members can offer valuable perspectives during monitoring visits

Assessing process quality also refers to interactions and the overall quality of instruction and care. When monitoring visits focus on processes, they often intend to examine the relations between staff and children and staff and parents, and collaboration within the staff team. Observation is increasingly used in other countries to monitor process quality, including curriculum implementation. In many countries, observations are combined with interviews with managers and staff as well (e.g. England [United Kingdom], Ireland, Norway).

Monitoring in Luxembourg relies heavily on the analysis of internal documents. Writing these documents requires knowledge and skills that can be different from those required from staff in their daily interactions with children; moreover, internal documents are usually put together by the leader of the setting, not always in collaboration with the staff. In addition, regional officers mainly talk to leaders of settings during their visits. Thus, the voices of those interacting with children in settings are mostly unheard, and actual pedagogical practices are currently not observed. To deepen the knowledge on process quality, there is a need to broaden the sources of information on quality available to the regional officers during their visits, in including meetings and discussions with staff members. Introducing systematic observations of staff and children during everyday activities would also deepen the knowledge on process quality.

As SNJ has revised the guidelines for monitoring procedures, the next step would be to ensure that these revisions translate into changes in practices during monitoring visits with an increased focus on collecting information on interactions through observations in settings, which is under consideration for the future. If implemented, there will need to be a clear description of aims, focus, and methods of observations to guide regional officers and ensure consistent procedures across monitoring visits. With the new monitoring framework under development, there is an opportunity to focus on how interactions support children's well-being and development.

Observed quality indicators are needed to substantiate the degree to which pedagogical intentions found in the pedagogical concept and logbook are related to observed staff behaviours that support children's development, including multilingual skills. For example, a focus on observing the quality of adult-child interactions could consider how adults engage in joint interactions with children and help them engage in communication and "sustained shared thinking" (Siraj, Kingston and Melhuish, 2015[17]). This includes adults not only observing and following children's lead and allowing for child-directed play but also enhancing children's creative play in setting up the environment and interacting in ways that provide opportunities for exploration in a context specifically designed to enhance language, development and learning. Relevant for the Luxembourg context and its multilingual education, for example, could be a focus on how adults model languages and engage children in extended exchanges and purposeful conversation, making use of a range of languages, including home languages where possible.

In continuing this new framework and the new tool for regional officers, a clear focus on interactions and on how interactions support children's well-being and development will be important, e.g. in terms of their social and emotional experiences, their developing socio-emotional skills, self-regulation and resilience. Indices on the use of multiple languages in daily life and in communications with parents need to be included. Quality indicators need to be included that are descriptive and not evaluative; it is the overall profile of strengths and challenges that can form the basis for a self-improvement plan.

Self-evaluation can guide improvement

Self-evaluations are increasingly seen as a key dimension to ensure the quality of provision in the ECEC sector, and there is a strong international trend towards developing policies and practices. ECEC leaders and/or staff commonly employ self-evaluations to assess their centre's level of quality (OECD, 2021[3]). Staff working directly with children are an important source of information on resources and support needed to provide good process quality. Self-evaluations can, for example, focus on collaboration in the team, communication and management, and assess what can be done to improve these aspects.

For settings under the ECEC subsidy funding system in Luxembourg, self-assessment procedures are mandatory and aim to strengthen discourse and reflection within the team, and thus lead to continuous improvement in quality (Achten and Bodeving, 2017[8]). In introducing self-evaluation into their quality assurance system, Luxembourg has recognised the value of promoting self-evaluation as one essential strategy to ensure quality. However, the results of self-evaluations are not currently used during monitoring visits, and little seems to be known about the resources and motivation of providers to engage in these processes, along with the impact these processes have on quality improvement. In response to this situation, a pilot project is currently ongoing. It tests a new self-evaluation tool developed by SNJ and made available to settings.

To ensure that self-evaluation leads to improvement, managers, leaders and practitioners in ECEC need to be provided with resources to help them build their skills and capacity to undertake effective self-evaluation and improvement planning in their own provision. External evaluators (in the case of Luxembourg, the regional officers carrying out monitoring visits) can play an important role in providing guidance on effective self-evaluation and improvement arrangements. The development of self-evaluation in ECEC settings can be led by those agencies in charge of external monitoring. Doing so will ensure that monitoring on both sides draws on the same standards and quality indicators.

Luxembourg is taking some important steps in this direction. Linked to the new framework for external evaluations and thus closely aligned with the curriculum and aiming to assess curriculum implementation, SNJ and MENJE are currently developing a framework and indicators for ECEC settings to guide their self-evaluation. Two issues need consideration here. First, to address differences in understanding of quality and adapt for different types of provision and contexts, it will be important to include the insider view of leaders and staff in settings to guide the development of such frameworks and tools. Luxembourg is currently planning small pilot studies, and feedback from participating settings will be an important step to ensure their voices are included. Second, to encourage reflection in the team and improvement of pedagogical practices and better implementation of the curriculum, it will be important that new tools for self-reflection ensure the involvement of ECEC staff with different backgrounds and experience in self-assessment processes.

Self-evaluation results can be part of external evaluation processes. They can be the starting point for external evaluators and provide leaders of settings, along with staff, with opportunities to share what they know about their processes and practices in relation to the key aspects of the review framework (OECD, 2021[3]). Luxembourg plans to introduce self-evaluation results as part of its external evaluation process. This is an important step and will help to better include the team's views on the quality they offer and the resources needed to improve quality. This is particularly relevant since Luxembourg's non-formal, non-contracted ECEC sector faces structural issues, with high staff turnover, high diversity in the workforce, and less favourable working conditions (see Chapter 2). These factors can make it difficult for staff to navigate resources and hinder their capacity for quality improvement.

Moreover, external evaluation processes can also help build staff capacity for self-evaluation if constructive dialogue and feedback on self-evaluation procedures and results are part of monitoring visits. Since Luxembourg is currently developing guidelines and tools for external and internal evaluations in parallel, this is an important opportunity to ensure that tools are aligned to complement each other and support bringing together information to facilitate shared reflections and improvement.

Mechanisms and strategies are needed to address children's diverse needs and interests

Monitoring of child development can also be part of internal evaluations, and children's actual experiences can be an essential focus of monitoring efforts (OECD, 2021[3]). Importantly, continuous and informal monitoring at the setting level may greatly help identify learning needs for staff and children, thus improving staff practices.

OECD countries have different views and take different approaches to monitoring child development; one common approach is the use of portfolios as a record of children's experiences and growth (OECD, 2021[3]). The measurement of child development and learning for very young children needs to be approached carefully. For diagnostic purposes and supporting additional needs, however, there is evidence on the benefits of naturalistic observations carried out on an ongoing basis (Meisels and Atkins-Burnett, 2000[18]). Luxembourg, therefore, might wish to consider introducing some mandatory documentation of individual children's engagement in learning experiences and their growth.

Considering the complexity of language profiles of children and staff in settings, and challenges with implementing a multilingual curriculum, a focus on monitoring individual children's multilingual learning experiences could be particularly useful. Other aspects of child learning that might be of relevance to non-formal education could also be considered, for example documenting children's collaboration, creativity and self-regulation. Sharing this information with parents would strengthen parent partnerships and how parents and ECEC providers can work together to respond to individual children's interests and needs (OECD, 2015[1]).

Making information on children's learning experiences and development available within a setting and to parents can also help identify when additional support mechanisms should be put in place. Results of such monitoring efforts could help ECEC settings receive additional resources to help address identified learning needs – for example, specially adapted equipment or specific additional services. A common approach in educational guidelines on early language learning in Europe concerns support for children who have *additional* needs in speech, language and communication. This is implemented by providing speech therapy or other kinds of specialist support on an individual basis or by staff receiving additional support or coaching from external support systems. For example, in Portugal, speech therapy can be provided to children who are at risk of poor outcomes and who need additional support; in Scotland, speech and language delay are identified as an area of need that entitles children to additional support; in Wales and Northern Ireland (United Kingdom), in areas that have been identified to have additional needs in speech, language and communication, programmes for children under 3 are targeted specifically at disadvantaged children (see EC/EACEA/Eurydice (2019[10])).

Parents and children should be engaged in monitoring quality processes

Surveys with parents can also be part of evaluations. They can provide parents with an opportunity to give their opinion on the level of quality and indicate their degree of satisfaction (OECD, 2015[1]). Monitoring results in Luxembourg are currently not used to address issues related to parental wishes and their level of satisfaction. Apart from regional officers receiving parent complaints to pass on, parents are not involved in the monitoring process, and internal collection of parent voices is not part of the mandatory quality assurance system. Parents, however, are valuable sources of information and can offer important perspectives on the perceived well-being of their children, their hopes and wishes for them, and concerns they may have about their children's well-being and development.

Luxembourg might want to consider involving parents in monitoring processes. For example, settings could be required to collect feedback from parents (for example, through parent surveys), and results of these efforts could be shared with regional officers during the monitoring visit. Optional evaluation tools could be developed to support settings in collecting parent feedback. In addition, selected parents could be given the opportunity to talk to regional officers during monitoring visits, and again the development of tools could support regional officers in this task. Europe, Croatia, Estonia, and Norway, for example, have developed standardised questionnaires to support ECEC settings in involving parents in their internal evaluations. In addition, standardised questionnaires for external evaluators have been developed in Montenegro and Scotland (for children under and over 3). Standardised questionnaires for parents that have been developed often ask for feedback on the following themes: co-operation and communication with parents, safety issues, the quality of children's learning and care and overall satisfaction. Other issues that can be addressed are: child well-being, adapting to children's needs, supporting transition and outdoor activities (EC/EACEA/Eurydice, 2019[4]).

In a number of European countries, formal parent bodies exist in individual centres for the whole age range in ECEC (including provision for children under and over 3), and parent representatives on the formal body have the right to participate in evaluation processes. How parents participate varies between countries; they can contribute to developing internal evaluation processes or discuss and approve evaluation reports. External evaluators can be required to check whether parents have had the opportunity to contribute to the internal evaluation of settings (EC/EACEA/Eurydice, 2019[4]). Luxembourg currently has plans to introduce a mandatory parent council for non-formal education at the national level. Another means to collect parent input would be to collect feedback from the parent council in response to the summary report of monitoring results.

Similarly, the voices of children participating in ECEC are a valuable source of information. Their perceptions of their own well-being and learning should be included in monitoring processes and inform decisions on ECEC. The importance of considering the view of children in monitoring the quality of ECEC has been established, but more needs to be done to develop methods that are appropriate and valid, especially with very young children (OECD, 2021[3]). In Europe, guidelines on the involvement of children in internal or external evaluation of ECEC are relatively common for children above the age of 3 or 4 but rare for children below 3. On an internal basis, regulations can require children to be involved in planning and assessing activities in ECEC on a regular basis (e.g. Norway), or settings can be required to use tools to gather children's views (e.g. Spain/Comunidad Valencia). Guidelines can also require external inspectors to speak with children of all ages about their views on the service and consider internal documentation of how children have been consulted (e.g. Scotland) (EC/EACEA/Eurydice, 2019[4]).

Regional officers can be further prepared and supported in their roles

To apply monitoring practices and tools with the depth of understanding needed and ensure that monitoring practices result in consistent and objective judgement, inspectors need to be trained, supported, and monitored (OECD, 2015[1]; Waterman et al., 2012[19]). Research findings suggest that training in implementing monitoring practices supports better monitoring practices, less bias in judgements and better capacity to use assessment for learning and development (OECD, 2015[1]).

In many countries, inspectors must participate in on-the-job or in-service training. Mandatory in-service training can be specified to a certain number of days per year (e.g. one to five days in Chile and Portugal or five to ten days in the Flemish Community of Belgium) (OECD, 2015[1]). In addition to in-service training, pre-service training can be required, and pre-service training can last several weeks (e.g. some *Länder* in Germany) or several years (e.g. England). Requirements for significant experience in early childhood development are rare (e.g. England), and so are requirements for external inspectors to have completed training in preschool education (OECD, 2021[3]; 2015[1]).

In Luxembourg, 32 regional officers have been recruited since 2017 and trained to perform monitoring visits in all non-formal settings, which are aligned with the quality framework. All regional officers have to have a master's degree in pedagogy or equivalent but do not necessarily have to have experience or training for work with children in education or ECEC specifically. Regional officers receive two months of initial training when they begin their roles.

Regional officers are monitored by two co-ordinators based centrally. Co-ordinators have received specific training and are regularly supervised. Regional officers and co-ordinators are in close communication, and working groups and further training opportunities are organised when the need arises. In addition, guidelines exist for regional officers on how to carry out their monitoring visits and on how to evaluate a setting's internal documentation documents (pedagogical concept, logbook).

Thus, Luxembourg has put several processes in place to ensure good quality evaluations. Nevertheless, the monitoring system is very young. During the interviews, stakeholders commented that there are challenges related to a shared understanding and vision on quality and how to arrive at sound conclusions with reference to the pedagogical and educational approaches of settings. Current efforts aim to build more consensus on several pedagogical issues, including participation, children's rights and the roles of the pedagogues. Selection and/or training requirements of regional officers could be expanded to include direct experience in ECEC provision. Further training for regional officers will need to focus on several issues, including the (shared) view on what good quality is and how it can be assessed. Here, tools for assessing process quality (for example, videos of differing levels of quality), which are closely linked to the curriculum framework, will be helpful. In addition, and considering that each regional officer has responsibility for many settings, it needs to be ensured that the administrative burden on regional officers is managed/balanced with their capacity to conduct visits.

The consequences and use of monitoring results

Context

Reports to the OECD review team mentioned that settings struggle to meet regulatory requirements in some areas and that it can be difficult for regional officers to address quality concerns. This suggests that the weaknesses identified through monitoring are not addressed with sufficient force to drive improvement across the entire sector, with some settings, often in the non-contracted sector, struggling to deliver the sophisticated child-oriented pedagogy and the multilingual curriculum.

In Luxembourg, the main aim of monitoring carried out by regional officers is to enhance the performance of ECEC provision. The results of monitoring visits are used to provide feedback, first to settings and second to SNJ and MENJE, on what works and to identify areas for improvement. First, at the end of their visit to settings, regional officers have a conversation with the leader of the setting. Their conversation style (open dialogues) and the monitoring methods aim to encourage exchanges throughout the course of their visits, which support the aims to deliver their developmental and support roles. Following their monitoring visits, and in addition to direct verbal feedback to leaders of settings, regional officers produce a report on the results of their visit, which is shared with the person responsible at the ECEC centre. Institutions are given the opportunity to comment on their report, and reports (including comments from the institution) are then shared with MENJE and the responsible person at SNJ.

Summary reports are produced, and if issues with the quality of provision are identified across several settings, shared discussions between relevant divisions under MENJE will take place to plan actions. Efforts are made to ensure that summary reports can more easily build on reports at the centre level. Recent issues that have been identified concerned curriculum implementation or staff understanding of multilingual education. Based on shared discussion and with the involvement of other stakeholders, monitoring results have in this way contributed to the recent revision of the curriculum framework, have led to changes in professional development programmes, and have influenced the planning of monitoring procedures.

Additional mechanisms could enhance the effectiveness of the monitoring system

Regional officers oversee the follow-up process with settings. The role of regional officers in providing support and driving improvement processes means that their monitoring results are (for the most part) not directly linked to consequences for settings. Further lowering stakes, individual monitoring reports are not made available to parents or children, and monitoring results are published in a summary report only. Nevertheless, if there are issues with a setting's compliance with legal regulations, regional officers are obliged to inform the Department for Children who can (if necessary) withdraw the ECEC subsidy funding scheme and thus the financial resources of the setting. In a case of continued breach of regulations, the setting can lose its licence and be removed from the register. However, as in other countries, and connected to demand and supply issues, non-compliance rarely leads to such high-stake consequences.

The range of options MENJE can take to ensure providers take action to address concerns may need to be revised. First, additional mechanisms to encourage settings to co-operate with regional officers could be considered to enhance the effectiveness of the monitoring system. With Singapore as a good example, some countries have introduced financial incentives for structures to design, implement, and monitor self-improvement plans (Box 3.2).

Box 3.2. Examples of incentivising quality improvement in ECEC settings: Singapore

Singapore supports quality improvement through its Preschool Accreditation Framework (SPARK), a monitoring system that places greater emphasis on improvement than on closure or punishment. It employs fiscal incentivisation to encourage participation in a quality improvement cycle, as Singapore has realised that meaningful and dramatic quality enhancement cannot be achieved without injecting substantial resources beyond conventional operating funds.

In Singapore, all ECEC centres must be inspected by the national agency every three years in order to hold operating licences. ECEC centres can also choose to participate in the SPARK process, which entails additional monitoring. Centres use the SPARK framework as a tool for self-assessment and planning, which is a precursor to the centre applying for external quality accreditation in centres catering to 4-6 year-olds. A SPARK quality scale for younger children is underway.

Singapore has invested substantial amounts of public funds in developing, trialling, implementing and evaluating its SPARK system. After extensive consultation with stakeholders, SPARK has developed its quality rating scale that includes observation and interviews with a range of staff as well as users. The aspects of quality, especially process quality, identified in their rating scale have been validated through international research, including the link between observed quality and children's developmental outcomes.

A significant component of SPARK is the development of a detailed improvement plan that includes leadership, planning, staff management, resources, curriculum and pedagogy. Like those in Korea, the quality inspectors in Singapore receive professional development related to observation, work to a visit template, and in the main have substantial experience of working in ECEC themselves. Their monitoring reports are constructive and thorough, containing clear steps towards improvement as well as a timetable for change. After a successful monitoring visit by national inspectors, the centre receives a "quality certificate", which, in turn, allows them to receive additional government subsidies.

Korea has a similar approach to incentivising centres to create, implement, and monitor self-improvement strategies, the consequences of which are monitored by external assessors. Thus, there is a close link between public accountability and public money in Singapore, as in its Asian neighbour, Korea. Each centre's SPARK report is accessible to parents and the public via the website and is used by parents in their choice of provider, much as government inspection reports are made public in Korea, Hong Kong (China) and England. Singapore considers the public sharing of monitoring data a vital element in their national policy of self-improvement and transparency, with more than 40% of preschools SPARK-certified.

Source: Bull, R. and A. Baudista (2018[20]), "A careful balancing act: Evolving and harmonising a hybrid system of ECEC in Singapore", in Kagan, S. (ed.), *The Early Advantage Vol 1: Early Childhood Systems That Lead by Example*, Teachers College, New York.

ECEC settings in Luxembourg are required by law to make their pedagogical concepts public. This is seen as a mechanism that enables parents to compare providers in terms of the pedagogical quality of a setting (Achten and Bodeving, 2017[8]). However, not all ECEC settings make their pedagogical concept public and there are currently no requirements for ECEC settings to make their monitoring reports publicly available. Luxembourg could introduce a requirement to publish (for example, on a parent portal) condensed information on the monitoring results (e.g. improvement plans and progress towards achieving goals, and if either parents or regional officers have raised issues for concern). From the side of regional officers or inspectors from the Department for Children, issues of concern could be non-compliance with regulations or settings not following up on recommendations. Such measures would help raise stakes and increase levels of transparency, especially for parents participating in the system. Ultimately, summary reports should be fully publicly available to inform parents, but there could be interim steps as tools, and the formats for reporting are currently refined.

The OECD (2021[3]) has recently highlighted the importance of considering the resources of monitoring systems needed to enhance the efficiency of monitoring processes, for example, by tailoring inspections according to the needs of providers. For example, the risk of low quality occurring in the future could be assessed during a monitoring visit, and upcoming visits for each setting could be adapted depending on the likelihood of continuing risks to quality. Such a risk-based inspection aims to ensure that the approach to inspection is proportionate and focuses efforts where they can have the greatest impact. One possibility to better channel resources is to introduce flexibility in the frequency of monitoring visits based on risk-based analysis. Limiting the number of visits each regional officer has to undertake would enable him/her to increase the depth of his/her work, e.g. include systematic observations in their visits, increase stakeholder involvement, and strengthen planning and action towards improvement. This approach could be particularly effective if combined with thorough self-evaluation processes and a review of self-evaluation results during each monitoring visit.

Second, additional mechanisms to support ECEC settings in Luxembourg to implement changes that have been recommended could be considered to enhance the effectiveness of the monitoring system. The "additional" mechanisms might include extra funding, as is done in Singapore (Box 3.2).

Importantly, monitoring can further contribute to quality improvement if monitoring results are shared with those institutions in charge of initial education of the ECEC workforce, as training can then be adapted accordingly to meet the professional and practical needs of future staff (OECD, 2015[1]). Strengthening communication channels between providers of continuous professional development training for ECEC staff and those dealing with monitoring results at MENJE could further improve the impact of monitoring results on quality improvement.

There are currently no systematic procedures in place for centre leaders to share monitoring results with staff members. Staff, however, are the main actors in delivering good quality ECEC. For monitoring to be effective in improving practice, assessment of practice needs to link up with the objectives for reflection and improvement, and ECEC staff need to be provided with feedback and support on how to use monitoring results for their development (OECD, 2021[3]). Thus, their involvement needs to be ensured not only during monitoring visits but also in designing improvement plans in response to the results of monitoring. Time during working hours also needs to be protected for any new required tasks.

The capacity of regional officers to foster quality improvement can be strengthened

Regional officers are not responsible for coaching managers and ECEC staff, but they are responsible for supporting providers to collaborate in the development of improvement plans. During interviews, challenges were reported concerning the task of regional officers in supporting quality improvement, and to some extent, these relate to ongoing challenges of developing a common understanding on important pedagogical issues. Hand in hand with the development of a common view on quality and those practices that support it, steps will need to be taken to support regional officers in making recommendations and drawing up improvement plans. The role of co-ordinators could, for example, be further developed to ensure regional officers have a consistent approach to quality improvement as well as quality assessment.

In addition, existing overlap in the functions of regional officers to support versus control may hinder the development of relationships of trust between regional officers and providers, which allows for effective collaborative processes in the development of improvement plans. Importantly, recent developments clarified the roles of officers and agents from the two monitoring bodies (SNJ and the Department for Childhood).

Regional officers need to be trained, well guided and supported on how to provide feedback to settings that is linked to their judgements and conclusions in monitoring reports. This requires transparency to staff in settings on how recommendations are linked to monitoring results. It also requires that regional officers are familiar with the quality support system and know how to match learning needs with those types of support available to staff in settings. Follow-up of improvement plans needs to be ensured, so that strategies are implemented in a timely manner, and evidence of effectiveness is collected and reviewed by regional officers. In response to these training needs, it is envisaged to make "job shadowing" during monitoring visits to centre-based and home-based providers part of the training for regional officers.

In addition, adopting a risk-based approach to inspection and limiting the number of visits by each regional officer would free up time to focus on developing quality improvement measures in consultation with ECEC settings. As a reform of professional development is ongoing, it will be important to better involve regional officers in professional development plans developed by settings (see Chapter 2). This reform provides opportunities to develop coaching and centre-embedded training that can be encouraged by regional officers to meet the needs for quality improvement of some settings.

Policies to improve performance in the ECEC sector can be more systematically informed by data on ECEC providers, children and the workforce

Planning of policies that ensure accessibility and quality of ECEC services requires analysis of performance in the sector that is based on and brings together information of its providers, workforce, and children and families. The linking of this quantitative data, together with outcomes of monitoring processes, can provide valuable evidence on the strengths and weaknesses of the ECEC system, which helps to identify gaps that need to be addressed, and thus plays a key role in guiding policy development.

In the context of Luxembourg, it will be particularly important to link findings on ECEC process and structural quality with analysis that assesses the diversity of participating families in relation to access and patterns of ECEC participation, and the diversity of the workforce, in relation to resources and working conditions in different types of provision. Research has shown that quality varies between different types of providers (e.g. Mathers, Sylva and Joshi (2007[21]); Slot et al. (2015[22])). The OECD review team has heard that this is also true in the context of Luxembourg, with the non-contracted sector and smaller centres, in particular, struggling to provide good quality ECEC and to comply with some regulations – for example, those related to staff language skills, or hours of professional development (see Chapter 2).

To understand if there is a need for an increase in public funding in the commercial (non-contracted) sector, or if tighter mechanisms need to be developed to ensure that resources are used efficiently to provide good quality, analysis of data on costs for ECEC providers is needed in relation to their receipt of demand-side subsidies (through the ECEC subsidy funding scheme) and their additional income through parent fees. Such analysis could help clarify if certain types of providers need additional supply-side funding, for example, those serving a higher percentage of children at risk (e.g. low-income families, children with additional educational needs or disabilities).

Bringing together data on each provider will also help monitoring bodies target their resources more effectively. A digital platform is currently being developed in Luxembourg with the aim to assist in centralising the collection of data, which should better enable the sharing and effective use of information. The aim is to integrate, for example, data collected through licensing processes and structural quality monitoring, as well as results from monitoring, focusing on process quality aspects. The integration of further quantitative data on enrolment, staffing and users of ECEC in this single database should also be considered. The design of a portal that integrates the infrastructure to receive public funding (e.g. subsidies through the ECEC subsidy funding scheme or funds for professional development) with the collection of information required for monitoring will reduce the administrative burden for providers while at the same ensuring data is provided, and can be linked to enable analysis that informs policies.

Steps will need to be taken to plan who contributes to the collection of this data, which resources are needed at the level of the centre or provider to ensure information is kept up to date, how arrangements of data sharing between relevant divisions can be set up, and who oversees analysis of this information to assess the performance of the sector and guide policy development.

A forensic review of early childhood services in six high performing countries (Australia, Hong Kong [China], Finland, Korea, Singapore, England [United Kingdom]) (Kagan et al., 2019[23]) identified several building blocks of effective systems, among which is included "data to drive improvement". This building block focused on strategies within each country to "advance knowledge, evaluate program effectiveness, test innovations, fuel strategic planning, and inform policy reforms". Deliberate and intentional processes in each of the successful countries to collect, synthesise and then use data on both children and services drive improvements across the system. Luxembourg's use of this building block, "data to drive improvement", needs review and strengthening to match the ambitious curricular aims of the country and its substantial financial investment.

References

Achten, M. and C. Bodeving (2017), "Development of quality in the non-formal education sector in Luxembourg", in Klinkhammer, N. et al. (eds.), *Monitoring Quality in Early Childhood Education and Care: Approaches and Experience from Selected Countries*, German Youth Institute, Department of Children and Childcare, Munich. [8]

Bull, R. and A. Bautista (2018), *A careful balancing act: Evolving and harmonising a hybrid system of ECEC in Singapore*, Teachers College, New York. [20]

de Haan, A. et al. (2013), "Targeted versus mixed preschools and kindergartens: Effects of class composition and teacher-managed activities on disadvantaged children's emergent academic skills", *School Effectiveness and School Improvement*, Vol. 24/2, pp. 177-194, http://dx.doi.org/10.1080/09243453.2012.749792. [14]

Early, D. et al. (2010), "How do pre-kindergartners spend their time?, Gender, ethnicity, and income as predictors of experiences in pre-kindergarten classrooms", *Early Childhood Research Quarterly*, Vol. 25, pp. 177–193, http://10.1016/j.ecresq.2009.10.003. [15]

EC/EACEA/Eurydice (2019), *Eurydice Brief: Key Data on Early Childhood Education and Care in Europe*, Publications Office of the European Union, Luxembourg, https://eacea.ec.europa.eu/national-policies/eurydice/content/eurydice-brief-key-data-early-childhood-education-and-care-europe_en (accessed on 6 October 2021). [4]

EC/EACEA/Eurydice (2019), *Eurydice Report: Key Data on Early Childhood Education and Care in Europe – 2019 Edition*, Publications Office of the European Union, Luxembourg, https://eacea.ec.europa.eu/national-policies/eurydice/content/key-data-early-childhood-education-and-care-europe---2019-edition_en. [10]

Eurofound (2012), *Quality of Life in Europe: Impacts of the Crisis*, Publications Office of the European Union, Luxembourg, https://www.eurofound.europa.eu/publications/report/2012/quality-of-life-social-policies/quality-of-life-in-europe-impacts-of-the-crisis. [13]

Kagan, S. et al. (2019), "Data to drive improvement", in Kagan, S. (ed.), *The Early Advantage: Building Systems That Work for Young Children, Volume 2*, Teachers College Press, New York. [23]

Kuger, S. and K. Kluczniok (2008), "Prozessqualität im Kindergarten, Konzept, Umsetzung und Befunde, Zeitschrift für Erziehungswissenschaft", *Sonderheft*, Vol. 11, pp. 159–178, http://dx.doi.org/10.1007/978-3-531-91452-7_11. [16]

Luxembourg Ministry of Education, Children and Youth (2020), *The Luxembourg Education System*, https://men.public.lu/dam-assets/catalogue-publications/divers/informations-generales/the-luxembourg-education-system-en.pdf. [9]

Mathers, S., K. Sylva and H. Joshi (2007), *Quality of Childcare Settings in the Millenium Cohort Study*, Research Report SSU/2007/FR/025, Department for Education and Skill, Nottingham, https://dera.ioe.ac.uk/8088/. [21]

Meisels, S. and S. Atkins-Burnett (2000), "The elements of early childhood assessment", in Shonkoff, J. and S. Meisels (eds.), *Handbook of Early Childhood Intervention*, Cambridge University Press, http://dx.doi.org/10.1017/CBO9780511529320.013. [18]

Melhuish, E. et al. (2015), "A review of research on the effects of early childhood education and care (ECEC) upon child development", CARE project, https://ecec-care.org/fileadmin/careproject/Publications/reports/CARE_WP4_D4__1_review_of_effects_of_ecec.pdf. [6]

OECD (2021), *Starting Strong VI: Supporting Meaningful Interactions in Early Childhood Education and Care*, Starting Strong, OECD Publishing, Paris, https://dx.doi.org/10.1787/f47a06ae-en. [3]

OECD (2020), *Quality Early Childhood Education and Care for Children Under Age 3: Results from the Starting Strong Survey 2018*, TALIS, OECD Publishing, Paris, https://doi.org/10.1787/99f8bc95-en. [12]

OECD (2018), *Engaging Young Children: Lessons from Research about Quality in Early Childhood Education and Care*, Starting Strong, OECD Publishing, Paris, https://dx.doi.org/10.1787/9789264085145-en. [2]

OECD (2015), *Starting Strong IV: Monitoring Quality in Early Childhood Education and Care*, Starting Strong, OECD Publishing, Paris, https://dx.doi.org/10.1787/9789264233515-en. [1]

Pascal, C. et al. (2013), *A Comparison of International Childcare Systems: Research Report*, Centre for Research in Early Childhood (CREC), Birmingham, https://assets.publishing.service.gov.uk/government/uploads/system/uploads/attachment_data/file/212564/DFE-RR269.pdf. [5]

Shuey, E. and M. Kankaras (2018), "The Power and Promise of Early Learning", *OECD Education Working Papers*, No. 186, OECD Publishing, Paris, http://dx.doi.org/10.1787/f9b2e53f-en. [7]

Siraj, I., D. Kingston and E. Melhuish (2015), *Assessing Quality in Early Childhood Education and Care: Sustained Shared Thinking and Emotional Well-being (SSTEW) Scale for 2–5-year-olds Provision*, Trentham Books, London. [17]

Slot, P., M. Lerkkanen and P. Leseman (2015), "The relations between structural quality and process quality in European early childhood education and care provisions: Secondary analyses of large scale studies in five countries", CARE Project. [22]

SNJ (2021), *Quality Beyond Regulations in Early Childhood Education and Care (ECEC): Country Background Report of Luxembourg*, Service national de la jeunesse. [11]

Waterman, C. et al. (2012), "The matter of assessor variance in early childhood education: Or whose score is it anyway?", *Early Childhood Research Quarterly*, Vol. 27/1, pp. 46-54, http://10.1016/j.ecresq.2011.06.003. [19]

Annex A. Programme of missions conducted by the review team

Table A A.1. Fact-finding mission (online), May-June 2021

Date	Institution
Monday, 17 May	
14.30-15.30	Service National de la Jeunesse (SNJ)
15.30-16.30	Service National de la Jeunesse (SNJ)
Tuesday, 18 May	
08.45-10.00	Service National de la Jeunesse (SNJ)
10.00-11.00	Quality Development Division - SNJ
Wednesday, 19 May	
10.00-11.00	Innovation division - further training - SNJ
14.00-15.00	Regional officers co-ordination - SNJ
15.00-16.00	International Relations division (Ministry of Education, Children and Youth - MENJE)
Thursday, 20 May	
10.00-11.00	Innovation division - plurilingual education - SNJ
14.00-15.00	Innovation division - publications / Site of www.enfancejeunesse.lu - SNJ
Friday, 21 May	
10.00-11.00	Service de l'éducation et d'accueil - MENJE
14.00-15.00	Ministère de l'Éducation nationale, de l'Enfance et de la Jeunesse (MENJE)
Friday, 25 June	
10.00-11.15	Researchers, University of Luxembourg

Table A A.2. Main mission, October 2021

Date (format)	Institution
Monday, 4 October (online)	
9.00-10.00	ANCES (Association Nationale Des Communautés Éducatives Et Sociales Du Luxembourg)
10.00-11.00	Service de la Formation Professionnelle - MENJE
14.00-15.00	Regional Officers
Tuesday, 5 October (online)	
9.00-10.00	LTPES (Lycée Technique Pour Professions Éducatives Et Sociales)
10.00-11.00	Multilingual Education Programme
11.00-12.00	Regional Officers Co-ordination
13.00-14.00	Direction générale du secteur de l'Enfance
14.00-15:00	FAPEL (Fédération Des Associations De Parents D'élèves Du Luxembourg)
Wednesday, 6 October (in-person)	
8.30-9.30	Agence Dageselteren
11.00-12.00	Further Training Division For Innovation - SNJ
13.00-14.00	Researchers - University of Luxembourg
14.15-15:15	FELSEA (Fédération Luxembourgeoise Des Services D'éducation Et D'accueil Pour Enfants)
15.30-17:00	ARCUS and CJF (Caritas Jeunes Et Familles)
17.00-18:00	National Inclusion Committee

Date (format)	Institution
Thursday, 7 October (in-person)	
8.00-9.00	Quality Development Division -SNJ
9.15-10.45	SNJ and Direction générale du secteur de l'Enfance
11.00-12.00	SCRIPT (Service de Co-ordination de la Recherche et de l'Innovation pédagogiques et technologiques)
13.30-15:00	ECEC setting visit
16:30-18:00	ECEC setting visit
Friday, 8 October (in-person)	
8.30-10.00	ECEC setting visit
11.00-12.30	ECEC setting visit
Friday, 22 October (online)	
10.00-11.30	Direction Générale de l'Enseignement Fondamentale

www.ingramcontent.com/pod-product-compliance
Lightning Source LLC
Chambersburg PA
CBHW082108210326
41599CB00033B/6633